Wording
the Silent Art

Wording the Silent Art

ESSAYS AND WRITINGS

BY BARBARA CARUSO

THE MERCURY PRESS

The publisher gratefully acknowledges the financial assistance of the Canada Council for the Arts, the Ontario Arts Council, and the Ontario Tax Credit Program. The publisher further acknowledges the financial support of the Government of Canada through the Book Publishing Industry Development Program (BPIDP) for our publishing activities.

Edited by Beverley Daurio
Composition and page design by Beverley Daurio
Printed and bound in Canada
Printed on acid-free paper

1 2 3 4 5 05 04 03 02 01

Canadian Cataloguing in Publication Data

Caruso, Barbara, 1937-
ISBN 1-55128-094-9
I. Title II. Series
N7445.2.C373 2001 709'.71 C2001-903002-9

The Mercury Press
Box 672, Station P, Toronto, Ontario Canada M5S 2Y4
www.themercurypress.ca

for Nelson

CONTENTS

Introduction

This book gathers a selection of my writings about art from the past 30 years. The pieces were written for different reasons and for different readers: sometimes for fellow artists, or for gallery curators; sometimes for writers, the readers of a literary journal; sometimes for the more general readers of art magazines, and sometimes for the readers of catalogues for exhibitions of my paintings and drawings.

Visual art is silent insofar as it does not use words; painting, in particular, is the silent art. Writing about art appears to be the province of critics and historians, but there is a tradition among artists, especially the modernist artists, of writing about their art. For some of us who read the modernist artists' writing, they are fine examples of what can be achieved in writing about difficult art; for others, they only confound or confuse.

The earliest writing included here is about my drawings. bpNichol asked me to write about my work for a TRG Report on narrative for *Open Letter*, and despite my protest— *I'm not a writer; I'm a painter!*— I conscientiously gave myself to writing "Telling About Line Telling." The piece is self-conscious and tenuous, but bp praised it and published it. I have revised this piece only slightly to preserve the original.

The "artist's statement" seems to have come into use with my generation. A short written statement by the artist was often posted on the wall of a private gallery in an exhibition of the artist's work. For group exhibitions, each artist might be expected to supply a brief statement about his work or his "philosophy." If a catalogue for the show was produced, these short statements were sometimes edited to one or two sentences. Readers of these statements complained that they were unintelligible. Often, they were. The few words in which an artist had struggled to say something meaningful were cut beyond recognition. Artists who lost heart wrote statements like: My work speaks for itself.

I wrote many of these statements and it was because of them that I learned that it was better to write long, but not too long, than to write short. My work is "abstract" or non-objective; I believe that all viewers can see and understand abstract painting if they give their time to looking and noticing. My earliest efforts at writing statements assumed that the reader/viewer would see what I had made simply because it was present. I learned that even the willing viewer wants a place to start, and often s/he wants it in words.

It was Nelson who told me to try to write about my work using as many words as I needed. It was a challenge and an exercise. The result was published as the catalogue essay for my exhibition, *Paintings 1969-1977*, at the Gallery/Stratford, and that essay became the model for "The Colour Lock Paintings 1969-1983." Both are included here. Together they show my struggle to word my own silent art.

I wrote reviews for a variety of reasons, often using a pseudonym. Sometimes I was asked to write by an artist, and I did. Sometimes I wrote to test myself, to prove that a show could be reviewed mentioning all of the artists and all of the works in it, or that a difficult show need not be passed over because it presented problems with wording. Sometimes I wrote a review for a show that had already been reviewed, but in a manner I thought was inadequate or an insult to the artist.

The eight essays that make up "A Letter from Paris" are included here. Gathered together, they seem tougher, more insistent, than when I wrote them. I make no apology, but when I read them through, I am struck by the extent of my audacity and (dare I say it) my courage in writing them. "A Letter from Paris" was written for a readership of artists who, I suspect, delighted in my irreverent criticism of the system under which we all labour.

I still maintain that I am not a writer. That I am a painter may have added something useful to two of the essays included here: the one about Barnett Newman's painting, *Voice of Fire*, and the other, *What Colour Are the Gallery Walls?* Descriptions of colour and light, what it is and how it works, are rarely attempted by art writers— not by art critics nor art historians.

What Colour Are the Gallery Walls? should not be read as a diatribe against the Art Gallery of Ontario. Rather, it is my strongly worded objection to the current practice of showing art in rooms with coloured walls in art museums everywhere. The AGO figures prominently in the essay because I visit it regularly and have been doing so since I was 18 years old. It is the first art museum I ever visited and I prize my memory of the exhibitions I have seen there. The AGO is *my* Gallery; in it, now, I mourn the loss of serious engagement and quiet contemplation of the art in rooms with coloured walls.

The essays on *Voice of Fire* and *What Colour Are the Gallery Walls?* were written because I did not see anyone else saying what I believed needed to be said. I complained to Nelson loudly and repeatedly— *This is not my job!* I wrote these essays not with a pen, but with a baseball bat because the job, when it fell to me, could only be done that way.

The collection, then, is highly personal and because of that I decided to include five personal letters. They were written to some of my dearest friends and a few good men who appear here anonymously (you know who you are).

I am not an easy writer for editors. I work hard to say what I believe; my words are hard-won. Just as I would not think of letting anyone change a stroke in my paintings, so I resist changes to what I have written. I am difficult, not impossible, but editors, too, have their styles.

I am grateful to bpNichol (1944-1988) for believing I could handle whatever writing project he proposed. He accepted what I wrote without questioning it, without editing it, giving me confidence in my eccentricities. I thank Judith Sandiford, editor of *Work Seen* (later, *Artword*) for her patience and for her good advice which I eventually took to heart. To Beverley Daurio, the laurel must be given, for without her care, this book would not be so. And always, there is my confidant, my reader, my poet, Nelson Ball, who has shared the past 36 years with me and doesn't want out yet.

July, 2001
Paris, Ontario

A Letter from Paris (1989-1991)

The Toronto Art Scene.

I moved from Toronto to Paris, Ontario, four years ago, but I still think of myself as a Toronto artist. After almost 20 years in Toronto, painting in its "ambience" and seeing its art scene grow and change, I am willing to grant Toronto's art community the right to declare itself a centre-of-the-world. I go to Toronto to learn what is happening there. I visit friends; I buy my supplies there, but mostly I visit the galleries.

It is not hard to keep in touch with Toronto. The city is only 75 miles away and I write letters. I write letters and receive replies from painters, sculptors and poets not only from Toronto, but also from Victoria, Edmonton, Montreal, New York and London, England, and occasionally I receive postcards with messages from that other Paris. I do not feel isolated here in my Paris any more than I felt isolated when I lived in Toronto. Painting is a lone job, an intensely concentrated act that is best sustained in solitude. If I am isolated, it is by choice, because painting is my most important occupation.

I live in a house with 30,000 books that fill the first and third floors of the building. The second floor (my domain) is filled with my work: my paintings, my drawings, my thinking and my books on art. I never lack a friend here because I can always find one in a book. Most of the books moved with me from Toronto. They, like me, are settling in to this place in Paris where there is more space, more time, better air, and the demon cost-of-living is finally de-fanged.

As a Toronto artist who no longer lives in Toronto, I am discovering that my view of the Toronto art scene is changing. While I lived there, I was able to see the undercurrents that propelled the flow of events. Now, removed from the activity of the scene, I see its ungarnished consequences. I have a privileged view now that I did not have before; it is more distant but clearer. I believe I can see the Toronto art scene in the way *it wants to be seen*. I am an objective observer, up close or from a distance; my subjectivity is my own affair.

Over the past year, I have been told by more than one Toronto art writer on more than one occasion that "nothing is happening" in Toronto. This idea amuses me. For me, something was happening because something is always happening. Interpretations and analyses may flag, but *something is always happening everywhere*.

Of course, Toronto has changed over the past four years. It is more a city of "haves" and "have-nots." The art scene, as always, is dividing and re-dividing into "somebodies" and "nobodies." In the art community, being somebody or doing something is very important. One can not be somebody for very long, and one can not be seen to be doing something for very long in Toronto. The art community is like a child with a short attention span. This creates a poor environment for a flourishing art. It is strange that the city should have so many artists in it.

An art community can be seen as a kind of system. The artists need each other and they need the galleries, the dealers, the curators and the art critics. The galleries show artists' work to other artists, to those people interested in art and to that great mass of people that has come to be called "the general public." In public galleries, I sometimes, but not often, meet other artists who are also viewing the shows I see; I see other quiet viewers (maybe they are artists, too, and I don't know it) whose silent presence I enjoy sharing. The general public who come to the galleries *en masse* are school children who are guided through the gallery by docents or teachers. They are very noisy. In the private galleries, I see few other viewers. This puzzles me. Why are there so few other willing viewers in Toronto's galleries whenever I am there?

I don't like to talk about a show I haven't seen. I don't like to talk about a show I went to see that didn't hold me, because I know that I did not give it a fair viewing. It takes time to see a show, and sometimes I return to a gallery to see the same show a second time. This doesn't necessarily mean that I *like* the show; it means I am interested by it. If I want to see more, I must look more. I see a lot of shows in Toronto that I don't like that interest me. Much of the art being shown does not want to be liked; it is didactic and pedantic. It intends by undisciplined means to discipline the viewer's mind and it is aimed at a general public. This art is both for the general public and about it. This art anticipates a viewer who is misinformed or uninformed or simply wrong-headed. If one has any doubts about this, there is ample information about it. That is the work of the curator-writer.

On my last trip to Toronto I saw the exhibition at S.L. Simpson Gallery called "The Anti-Graceful," curated by Bruce Grenville. I could not enter this exhibition entirely without prejudice because I had read John Bentley Mays' review of the show in the *Globe and Mail* ("Feeble Works no 'threat' to Modernism," Saturday, May 27, 1989). I was not influenced by Mays' review, but I had been informed by it of that reviewer's opinion of the curator's motives in bringing this show together. There were five artists on exhibit, but it was the curator's show.

Grenville had prepared a printed hand-out that gave the interpretation of modernism he wished to address. The opening paragraph, his general thesis, was almost unintelligible but I found, after a second reading, that it was current. There followed a more particular commentary about making bad art with authority under the heading of each artist's name, and a brief description of how each artist had achieved it. The hand-out was a difficult read and it was clearly intended to be seen before the exhibition.

The exhibition was an installation and Grenville, the curator, appeared to have taken on the role of the installation artist. The works by the five artists (Abraham David Christian, Tom Dean, Janice Gurney, Carol Laing, Mary Scott) were as "found" objects which articulated the thesis Grenville wished to present. This gave the exhibition the overall gracelessness Grenville wanted, and it impaired the separation of each artist's works. The stenciled work by Carol Laing helped to achieve the *pot-pourri* effect for not only did it fill one wall (one stencil repeated nine times), but fragments of the stenciled image decorated the other walls above and around the other artists' works. However, I was able to separate each artist's contribution.

Christian's sculptures best fulfilled the parameters of Grenville's "anti-graceful" theory by being pretentiously graceful and empty of all meaning. That they should be so did not interest me very much. They were a calculated synthesis of a current interpretation of modernism which I don't find convincing. Christian, however, must be convinced of it, and his work stood in this show as Grenville's star performance. The Laing stencils seemed out of place both as modernism and as decoration. The "domestic" and "commercial" referents implicit in Laing's choice of stencil design, and in Grenville's choice of Laing, did not well serve a serious challenge to modernism.

Dean's, Scott's and Gurney's works participated uncomfortably in Grenville's exercise (or should I say *exorcize*). Gurney's work, in particular, engaged me in ways that Grenville would not imagine. I had seen this series, *Interpretation of Vida and Myself*, before. If memory serves me, I saw it a few years ago at YYZ Gallery when it was on Spadina Avenue. Grenville believes "there is an embarrassing gap between the promise of representation and the resulting images" in the six works. But Grenville is pedantic and for him, process is academic and the academic is everything. I believe that these works should not be seen in Grenville's anti-graceful context because it diminishes what Gurney has achieved. (I don't know what Janice Gurney would say about this.) The "gap" that Grenville is so embarrassed by in these works exists only in his mind. He is a subjective viewer who extrapolates from the first suggestion that comes to his mind on seeing a painting; he is a reactionary steeped in traditional associations of portraiture. Grenville tosses about the words "lived experience," but he does not seem to know what that is for the artist, in the art, or for the viewer.

Only a misinterpretation of modernism can deny its *lived experience*. Grenville has built his thesis on a false premise. He has represented his thinking by presenting five artists' works. Do these artists believe they have been well represented under Grenville's banner? Perhaps they all do, for I hear no protest from those who were chosen. Grenville's installation denigrates the art it presents as a challenge to modernism. The show is a successful failure, a rational absurdity, and its sentiments are appropriately embarrassing to its curator. I did not like this exhibition, but I thought it was very very interesting. It represents the Toronto art scene as it wants to be seen.

1989

Artists' Writing and Critics' Writing.

It appears that "modernism" has become the subject of new scrutiny. Modernism, in this case, is described as the art made in Europe between the turn of the century and 1945. Of course, this art has been the subject of certain scholarship for decades; however, in the present climate of art criticism engendered by the academic study of popular culture, modernism is again in the hands of the Philistines.

It would seem that the critics make little distinction between "abstract" and "non-objective" art. Both share the same characteristic— they are non-figurative or non-representational. It is this characteristic that strikes the viewer/critic as irrational. This characteristic has always confused viewers. In fact, any divergence from a viewer's concept of his own observed reality can disturb him. As a result, certain forms in modernism have been described in the past as distortion, or as surrealism, or, more unfortunately, as a negation of reality, an attempt to destroy rather than create.

This negative understanding of modernism has been applied to cubist painting, to Dada, and to Futurism. It accounts for reams of art writing which blight the minds of art history students who study it assiduously. (Notice, Reader, that the art history student studies, not the art, not the writing of modernist artists, but the writing of critics and art historians.) Historians who take as their subject the De Stijl movement or the Russian avant-garde most often describe the artists who created these advances in perception as "utopian" or as idealists engaged with "absolutes." This is the consequence of the historians' lack of vision.

I, too, read the art historians' treatises, and I also read the writings of modernist artists. Some modernist artists who wrote about their art have been called "theorists." This is a poor label; it would be better to call them *observers*. Artists are observers in the sense that scientists are observers, and just as the scientist is compelled to invent ideas which will correspond to the reality of our world, the artist in his writing tries to build concepts which will correspond to his perception, his grasp of the reality of his world. The writings of modernist artists are considered to be abstruse, obscure, and sometimes confused or nonsensical by some historians who study them.

There is a vast difference between the writing of artists and that of art historians. The historians survey art and formulate generalities about it. These generalizations, however true they may appear, become useless when applied to the particular of painting or of sculpture. Compare this to the modernist artist who articulates in words those particulars of art and nature which he has observed and which he creates in his art. The historians write long analyses to classify and compartmentalize some fragment of visual experience. The artist, on the other hand, writes in a simpler language (borrowed, as it must be, from the vocabulary at large) to build an idea, reveal an insight that he has seen and understood and wants to make known. The artist's writings are often short texts as dense as texts written by philosophers.

The historians' approach keeps conventional thinking intact, and adds to it evidence of some "influence" (previously overlooked) which will change the established pattern slightly, but never too much. The modernist artist who wrote did so to explode the boundaries of conventional thinking and make room for the discoveries of his art. Some modernist artists wrote very careful, rational texts (Kandinsky, Mondrian); others sometimes wrote with impassioned extravagance (Van Doesburg, Malevich) in their impatience with the critical conventions of their time. The historians' writing is analytical; it separates ideas and examines them one by one. The artists' writing is intended to be *revelatory*. I consider the artist to be a builder-upper; the historian, a tearer-downer.

I believe that every art history student, as well as every artist, would do well to pore over the writings by modernist artists until they grasp the perception the artists have tried to reveal. If this were achieved, modernist art would no longer be a mystery even for those who find themselves attracted to it. Modernist art is not about words (concepts); it is a visual event which surpasses the fixed constructs of the popular mind. This was true between 1900 and 1945; it is still true today.

I am a painter, Reader, and you may have noticed that my argument is already a classic one— for centuries those who make art have opposed the intrusion of misrepresentations of art by non-artists. While art has its history, so also does art history have its history. It is important for artists to know what the historians are saying; it is imperative that critics and historians know what artists are saying both by their words and in their art.

Over the past decade, art criticism has taken on a new self-proclaimed authority. It has brought to its arsenal the ideas and vocabulary of literary criticism, of structuralism, semiotics, deconstruction— new analytical tools that make self-conscious formulae of mass media and popular culture. The methodology is not bad in itself, for it raises questions about fixed responses to art forms whose purpose is to persuade or manipulate the unconscious mind. However, with these means, the art critic has withdrawn from his role of examining art and instead, he examines the unconscious mind of the art viewer. The critic, now more comfortably allied with the mind of the average viewer (or the general public), has abandoned the artist as a creator. The artist has been marginalized to such a degree that he is said to have no existence and his art, no meaning— this, at least, is the position taken by the critic. In his bid for self-aggrandizement, the critic declares that art, in itself, is meaningless, that it is only through his own and his colleagues' interpretations that it is given meaning.

This misguided development has had a useful role to play over the past decade. In the same period, a new figurative art emerged, an art that is motivated by subjective reactions to issues that have been represented in the popular media and are current in the popular mind. Feminist concerns, Marxist theory, nationalism, political ideologies, gay rights, threat of nuclear war, consumerism and advertising, AIDS— all have been the focus of visual representation. Artists who share these concerns have made their positions manifest in their art, and the art writers have been able to analyze and interpret their images and extrapolate from them. All of this has been of great interest to me as a viewer of current art and a reader of current critical theory because I, too, have populist concerns— I just don't make a populist art.

To achieve authority for the unconscious populist mind, these artists and their critics had to declare another art dead— they called it "formalism." (Do you remember, Reader, when formalism was buried by "transavantgardism" from Italy, "neo-expressionism" from Germany, and then by all manner of "neo-neos" from the U.S.?) The formalism that was supposed to be put to rest in the early 1980s is a category of the modernism that is under attack now. Although I agree that it is fair to let each dog have its day, I think we are now into serious business.

I believe that modernism is the legacy of all living artists. It is our inheritance; it is the foundation of our work whether we acknowledge it as such or not. It is a legacy so vast that we have not begun to "spend" it. It lies like diamonds on the ground and we have barely begun to notice. We use this legacy even when we don't know that we are using it, and through this use we are informed by it and can discover its meaning. Modernism is about consciousness in the world. Until we see it, grasp it— and I mean grasp *all of it*— we cannot proceed as artists. If we do not proceed, we will leave no legacy for those who will inherit from us. We will have left only a *dark age*.

Modernism in its many forms was not popular in its own time nor at any time since. It is not meaningless; rather, it is difficult for the popular mind to grasp. Modernist art does not persuade or manipulate the viewer; the viewer either opens his mind to it or he is left untouched by it so that he might pass on to some other form of art that pleases him more. In a world as varied as our own, surely there is room for everyone and every form of art.

The current attitudes of art criticism discount the conscious mind of the artist and discredit art. When the art critic, like the uninformed viewer, looks at modernist art, he sees *nothing happening*. He searches his mind for signs and symbols, referents, metaphors, and if he can't find them, he makes them up. (It is possible to make a sow's ear out of a silk purse given certain assumptions.) The critic's approach is subjective and with his first thoughts he looks at himself, not the work of art that is in front of him. These thought processes make the critic singularly incompetent as an interpreter of modernist art.

I have said that modernism is again in the hands of the Philistines. Why do I say this? The answer lies in modernist art's own history, and it is not to be taken lightly.

Russia, 1922— Stalin was appointed secretary general and the suppression of modernist artists and writers began. Germany, 1933— Hitler became chancellor and the Weimar Republic was displaced. Modernist artists fled these countries or were persecuted for their "degenerate" art. A careful look at these events in modernist art's history points, not only to the facts of Communist or Nazi regimes, but more importantly to *the decline of liberalism and humanist values*. It is also worth noting that in each case the denigration of modernist art was done with popular approval; that is, the people (the general public) were persuaded that this art was meaningless.

It is hard in the complacency of our own time to draw parallels between ourselves and those repressive regimes, but the fact that we are experiencing a renewed conservatism, and have been witness to it over this past decade, should sound an alarm. The decline of liberalism and humanist values over this period has provoked protest from many areas of society, not least among them those artists who have turned their art to its purpose. But they are muted by other, more powerful factions who discredit and discount them.

The present challenge to modernism is being launched by art critics and historians whose minds, by their own admission, have never been open to it. They have nothing of value to say about it. They are truly the Philistines of this scenario, and their power to persuade the viewers of art, already confused by jargon, makes them a formidable enemy of every serious artist. It is time for artists to make their presence and their art known. It is time for painters, sculptors, visual artists of every discipline, to write down their thoughts and their impassioned insights again. We must hold on to our legacy and let no one cheat us out of what is ours.

1989

The Costakis Collection.

In May of this year, I went to Montreal to see the exhibition, *The Russian and Soviet Avant-garde: Works from the Collection of George Costakis*, at the Montreal Museum of Fine Art. It was not the first time I had seen the Costakis collection; I saw the exhibition at the National Gallery in Ottawa in 1982. I saw that exhibition over three days and I remember that when I left each time my head was spinning with new images and new names. Each day, I looked at everything in the show trying to grasp the individual pieces of work and the big idea that had to be at work in this surprising collection of art.

The exhibit in Montreal this year was a smaller selection than the one in Ottawa. The whole exhibit was well presented to bring emphasis to each artist and to the chronology of the works. I had two days to spend in Montreal and I spent both of them in the Museum looking at the show. It was a grand and exciting experience for me and this time I came away rewarded.

It will not be easy for me to define what was so important about seeing this collection again. It may be impossible for me to put into words the insights I believe are embodied in the work I saw. I don't intend to make this letter a review of the show, but I will try to articulate some of the thoughts that seemed clear to me as I viewed the show and those that have occurred to me since.

I have been interested in Russian modernist art for almost 20 years. Over that time, I have been able to see very little of it simply because the works that I knew existed were not where I could see them. I have read about this period in art history, and I have looked at reproductions of works in books and catalogues. I have pored over translations of statements and documents written by the artists active in the movement, trying to understand the scope of their vision. I have read about the politics of the period, the Revolution and the ideologies that created it. I have looked into the scientific revolution that changed the view of our world at about the same time as the artists in Russia leapt into a non-objective world. You may think, Reader, that I was well prepared to see this exhibition, but I know that I was armed mainly with secondary texts which familiarized me with prevailing ideas about what we, in Canada, loosely call "constructivism." Because I had not seen much of the work, and certainly not the Costakis collection, everything I had known about the Russian avant-garde was little more than rumour.

All critical evaluations of modernism suffer from the same problem, that is, lack of sufficient evidence. This makes it as difficult to support modernist art as it is to malign it. It makes little difference to the strength of each argument that the detractors select a narrow interpretation, while the supporters of modernist thought and art proclaim the breadth and openness of it, if neither side has seen (witnessed) the work.

The work in the Costakis collection was made between 1904 and 1930. The collection was first shown in North America in 1981. It has taken some 50 to 80 years for artists on this continent to be able to see these works. If this collection is new for our own generation, it was unknown to all the generations of artists since the 1920s. The developments outside Russia from 1917 onward occurred without the benefit of the *scope* of the Russian experience. Now, and only now, we have an opportunity to see a body of work made at a time when what we call modernism was in full flower, and this work is perhaps its most stringently conscious manifestation.

There were Russian artists who left Russia in 1921 and 1922—Kandinsky and Chagall (not in this exhibit) were among them. Kandinsky's art informed and was informed by this Russian movement, and what we see in this collection now will add to what we see in Kandinsky's work. Chagall's early work may be reconsidered in the light of this new evidence, for we know that this mysterious artist played a role in the cultural reconstruction in Russia after the revolution.

Because the Russian avant-garde movement is historically linked to the Russian Revolution, the artists are sometimes believed to be political revolutionaries. I think the artists were socially committed people, but their art was not politically motivated. It should be remembered that this art was made and shown first as a declaration of a new consciousness, then after 1917, as representative of cultural reconstruction, then after 1922, as the vehicle of social reform. It is not unusual for artists of any generation or era to want to make a difference or to contribute to a better world.

Critics and historians sometimes like to remove modernist art and thought from reality; they define it as an idealized view of the world. This satisfies even those critics and historians who would support modernist art. Among artists, it is this classification that is considered to be most misleading, because those artists who protest it insist upon the validity of the modernist view of the *real*. We debate, then, not from two different positions, but with two different minds.

In the Costakis collection, it is possible to see all of modernism contracted into those hidden years— from an impressionist through to a non-objective and an abstract art. Now that the collection is available for wider viewing and study, our understanding of modernist art and thought will be expanded by it. These works show so much that was previously unseen, unknown and unsuspected, that our knowledge of modernism will be changed by them. It will take time, of course, for it to be absorbed, but it will happen.

The work that most interests me in the Costakis collection is that made before 1922, before constructivist and productivist motives overtook its ideology. It was in 1921 that the group INKHUK determined that painting alone was not able to reach the sensibility of the proletariat, and a new constructivist effort was made to create a relevant utilitarian art modelled on the integrity of the pure art form that had developed in the previous years. This does not mean that artists stopped painting; rather, painting became less prominent and design and architecture were put into service in its place.

The Montreal exhibit showed seven works by Kazimir Malevich (1878-1935). The most directly Suprematist among them was *Black Quadrilateral*. I spent a long time looking at this small (6 3/4" x 9 1/2") painting and I noticed, for the first time, that the black shape is not an orderly rectangle— its sides are not parallel. This can't be seen clearly in reproductions of the work; it is as if the photographer has tried to correct Malevich's slightly irregular shape. I don't believe that Malevich made this shape in error; rather, I understand it as a particular order which may be seen to deny that theory that accounts for the non-objective image through geometry and for "geometric" art as symbolism.

It was the work of Ivan Kliun (1873-1942) that confirmed that thought for me. The collection is rich with Kliun's work— there were 37 pieces by him. Kliun, a mature artist at the time these works were made, a friend to Malevich and the older of the two men, is represented by works that explore colour and order, regular and irregular shapes, and their interrelationships. Kliun's works throughout 1917 unequivocally address the two-dimensional plane. Kliun achieves this by attaching the shapes on the plane to the painting's edge. The paintings from 1920-25 seem to address colour and light, and in the spherical compositions and constructions (the choice of word in the titles is important), I could not help thinking about the work of Robert Delaunay. If there was one artist I saw in the Ottawa show that made me want to see the Costakis collection again in Montreal, it was Ivan Kliun. I think Kliun's work gives an important clarification to Suprematism.

There are a surprising number of women artists among the Russian modernists. This fact should dispel the idea held by some feminist artists and most male artists that "formalism" has never attracted women artists. Instead, what we learn from the Costakis collection is that women and men, both young and old, worked together in Russia exploring, debating, arguing, drawing and painting and constructing with single-minded dedication.

Liubov Popova (1889-1924) is a model modernist by her work in this collection. Her drawings from 1913-14 show her dissolving the figure by exploiting its structure and energy; her paintings of 1914-15 show her working through cubism; from 1916 to 1921 she explores "painterly architectonics"— something closely allied to Suprematism— and these works most reveal a non-objective consciousness. From 1922 onward to her untimely death at 35, she worked on stage design, textile design and book and magazine designs where the utilitarian imperative of constructivism and productivism preoccupied her work. A study of Popova's work alone,

I think, could do much to clarify this revolutionary and revelatory art. Popova was a young woman throughout her entire life as an artist.

Because this collection has been lifted whole out of the past, no serious damage has yet been done to it— criticism has had no chance to eliminate the women artists, or to choose its heroes by dismissing some artists and championing others. The evidence of the Costakis collection as it is being made public is as startling to the eye and mind as the opening of King Tut's tomb must have been.

There were only two paintings by Mikhail Matiushin (1861-1934) in the exhibit, and one drawing by Elena Guro (1877-1913) was hung beside them. In the same room were hung the works of Matiushin's students, Nikolai Grinberg and the four Enders (Boris, Ksenia, Mariia and Yurii). This work, produced between 1918 and 1927, is committed to painting and to colour. Made through a period when the sensibility of the proletariat was of concern to many other artists, this work is based upon a highly esoteric concept of visual perception that has yet to be studied in its entirety. Matiushin's *Zorved* ("See/Know") has been described as "a system of scientific enquiry," but it is so original in its conception that it has not begun to be understood.

In 1913, Matiushin collaborated with the poet Kruchenykh on the opera *Victory Over the Sun*. Malevich designed the set and costumes. This opera (in my opinion) is a seminal work; it is *the* work that announced a new vision and consciousness to a public that was unwilling to take it seriously. The opera was ridiculed. Most of the artists in the Costakis collection were on the scene to see this opera, participate in it, or take part in the discussions around it. Today, I know only a few artists who have an interest in Malevich as a painter; I know no painters who know who Kruchenykh is, and I have only ever seen one reference to Matiushin by another painter— his name appears in a small painting by Greg Curnoe that I saw at the Yarlow/Salzman Gallery when it was on Richmond Street several years ago. Matiushin was a mature artist and a musician throughout the entire period of the Russian avant-garde movement. His work and his writings are a stone that cannot be left unturned. If we intend to address modernism in this post-modern age, we cannot afford to *not* see and *not* know these things.

An individual's view of the world will depend upon how much of his world he is conscious of, or how much he notices. That same individual's view of art will depend on what he *sees,* and what he *knows* of what he sees. His view of art will be the same as his view of nature, and he will see his own nature in it. Those who decry modernism cannot find themselves in it; they know only their own pasts and model the future on that. Those who find meaning in modernist art do so in its presence.

1989

Abstraction-Geometry-Painting. The exhibition.

Last November, I went to Buffalo to see the exhibition *Abstraction-Geometry-Painting* at the Albright-Knox Art Gallery. I had learned of this show from John Bentley Mays' review of it in the *Globe and Mail* ("Taking a walk on the austere side of abstract painting," Saturday, October 7, 1989).

The Mays review raised my expectations. His mention of "little-known pioneers of the 1930s such as Burgoyne Diller, Ilya Bolotowsky, Fritz Glarner and Charmion von Wiegand" gave me the impression that American avant-garde painters of the 1920s and 1930s would be shown, and at last, notice had been taken of the role they had played in establishing international art on the American scene. These artists may have been pioneers in a cultural wilderness, but they were also purveyors of modernist thought to the United States in the early decades of this century. Some of these artists gathered to found the American Abstract Artists (A.A.A.) in 1937, and I had hopes of seeing, for the first time, the works of Raymond Jonson, Stuart Walker, Rosalind Bengelsdorf, Balcomb and Gertrude Greene, Carl Holty, or Jean Xceron, among others, about whom I know so little. Mays' review raised the conundrum about Barnett Newman—his work is given great importance in American abstract art, and while a large part of the catalogue essay is given to it and its influence, it is not in the show. This, by Mays' report, was due to the unfortunate choice of one of the words in the title for the show—Geometry.

The word "geometric" has been used by some artists to describe the forms or shapes in non-objective painting and sculpture. It is a metaphor for the shapes (circle, triangle, square, quadrilateral) on the painted plane, or for the surfaces and multi-surfaced closures (cubes, cones, spheres) that may occur in sculpture. The vocabulary of geometry is descriptive, not only of shape, but of surface, when it presupposes planar event. However, when a painting is mistaken as a metaphor for geometry, the artist protests with good reason. All manner of confusion follows— from ideas about calculation to a pretence of symbolism, and most important for the painter, to the complete abnegation of colour. *All painters paint paint and that paint is coloured.* It is the fault of spoken language that the idea of *shape* and the idea of *colour* must be expressed by two separate words, even when they are perceived as *one thing* in nature and in painting. The non-objective or abstract painter decries the word "geometry." It is a red herring across the course of modernist art and critics have been sniffing at it to no good end for far too long. It was with much curiosity and some misgivings that I went to Buffalo.

I will not mislead you, Reader; my afternoon at the Gallery was a marvelous adventure. The show was beautiful. I spent all my time in the special exhibition galleries while my friend and driver, Linda Woolley, surveyed the Gallery's permanent collection. By the end of the day, my eyes were so full of what I had seen, and my mind so preoccupied with it that my driver had to steer me out the door, point me toward the parking lot and tell me to get into the car.

The earliest works in the show were by those four artists named in Mays' review. There were two paintings by Burgoyne Diller done in 1945 and 1964. Ilya Bolotowsky's 1960 tondo was shown, and a 1969 square painting hung on the diamond called *Scarlet Diamond*— yellow, blue and white shapes and a red ground shape. The tondo, called *Small White Tondo*, is all that its title suggests and its white shapes are separated by "lines." The "whites" can be seen to separate again as red-whites, yellow-whites and blue-whites. I was very interested by this small work. Fritz Glarner's *Rational Painting* (1943) and *Rational Painting #93* (1962) were shown. The span of 20 years between the two works attests to Glarner's tenacity and to the success of his pursuit. The earlier work (red, yellow, blue, black, two greys and a white ground) shows regular shapes horizontally and vertically disposed. In the later work (perhaps 91 paintings later), Glarner has retained the formal relationship of the shapes to the painting's edge, but the shapes are irregular (each shape has one oblique side), and no shape can be called a ground shape unless all shapes together be so called. The use of an oblique here invites a "movement" on the surface which the whole configuration denies. The one work shown by Charmion von Wiegand was *The Wheel of the Seasons* (1957). I believe that all of these artists are dead now. I did not have to be told that the choice of these particular works would point to Mondrian (not shown). Mondrian moved to New York in 1940 and became a member of the A.A.A. I was mildly disappointed that more work by these and other artists from the earliest years of American advanced art was not present. Because the selection was limited to "Geometric Abstract Painting... Since 1945," the foundation of the American non-objective consciousness was not well represented.

I found Josef Albers' and Ad Reinhardt's paintings in other rooms. These two artists had been members of the A.A.A. One of Albers' *Homage to the Square* paintings hung beside one of his two-centred colour paintings, and *Either... Or* (1948), another two-centred work, showed only white and four grey tones working the plane. These three Albers paintings alone would confirm that "geometry" is at best a metaphor, and that colour *at work* is the driving force in non-objective painting—even when those colours are black, white and grey.

The five Ad Reinhardt paintings included *Abstract Painting* (1948), a planar configuration dominated by secondary colours. *Red Abstract* (1952), *Blue Abstract* (1953) and *Abstract Painting* (1963), a "black" work, all show Reinhardt working with red, yellow and blue increasingly *reducing the light* until the colours are so dark they can only be called black. But even in the "black" painting, I could still see the primary colours at work on the surface.

There were several artists in the show whose work was completely new to me: John McLaughlin, Michael Loew, Myron Stout, Ludwig Sander, Jo Baer and John M. Miller. But I am a Canadian who rarely leaves this country so I fail to see whatever art this country doesn't show me. I determined to buy the catalogue for the show before leaving the gallery. The catalogue was as touted as the show in Mays' review, and I expected to cure my ignorance with it.

Leon Polk Smith showed two works, *Stone Wall* (1956) and *Three Yellow Ovals* (1967). I noticed that both of them were borrowed from the collection of the artist and I wondered about that. I was curious about the small black and white oil painting by Myron Stout. The two Michael Loew paintings held me for a long time. This artist had laid lean white paint over intense colour shapes to hold them to the white ground shape. This interested me greatly because I understood what I was seeing as *increasing the light*, or as an antithesis to Reinhardt's work.

There is a tendency for curators to hang look-alike paintings beside each other. This points out certain similarities of appearance, but it also can defuse the differences between them and lead the casual viewer to a faulty conclusion. Of the seven works shown by Ellsworth Kelly, the earliest were *La Combe III* (1951) and *Kite I* (1952), made while Kelly lived in Paris, France. These were hung for their look-alike qualities with the Glarner and Diller paintings. This could be misconstrued, for Kelly was not a member of the A.A.A. and was not in New York in those years. Kelly's large painting *New York, N.Y.* (1957) trumpets his home-coming. It exposes the huge letters N and Y, emphatically declaring white ground as figure and black figure as ground. However, in the course of the day, I overheard a docent telling a group of children in front of this painting to look for buildings, church-spires, flags and pennants in it and, oh yes, the letters N and Y. Kelly's oblique *Blue, Yellow, Red* (1968) and *Chatham #11, Blue/Yellow* (1971) were shown with his *Charter* (1959). These large works were hung in the largest gallery along with Gene Davis' *Citadel* (1962) and four paintings by Frank Stella made from 1959 to 1969. Here I began to wonder why more recent works by these artists were not also in the show. I know about Kelly's most recent work with irregular shapes and I wondered why it was not here, too. These artists are *not* dead. The works shown should not have been restricted to one or other decade; rather, in the context of "abstract" or "geometric" painting in America since 1945, the work by these artists is proof that such concerns among serious painters have reached into the 1980s and are reaching into the 1990s.

Two paintings from the 1960s by Kenneth Noland hung in a gallery with three 1960s paintings by Richard Anuszkiewicz and two works by Al Held (1968 and 1973). In another gallery, works by Robert Mangold hung beside a *Golden Section Painting* (1974) by Dorothea Rockburne, which hung beside a 1970 painting by David Novros. The Jo Baer painting, *Untitled* (1972-75), brought to my mind the epithet "minimalist" which, like "formalist," doesn't really mean much. In the same gallery were hung Brice Marden's *Red Yellow Blue Painting #1* (1974) and *Number Two* (1983-84) which showed not usual mixtures of the three complementary colour pairs, each painted in three verticals with the complement at the centre and horizontally at the top on three canvases that abutted to form one large work of immediate colour and surface. This painting and Mangold's *Three Colour Frame Painting* (1986) represented "geometry" in the 1980s in this show. It seemed to me that the show had been selected, not to survey the art of those painters represented, but to survey certain Survey Shows that have propelled the American art viewer from one style to another over the past 30 years. I could see Greenberg in this and I did not like it.

I found Larry Poons' *Orange Crush* (1963) beside John M. Miller's *Number Two* (1976); I found Agnes Martin's two works (1965 and 1977) across from Michael Loew's and John McLaughlin's paintings, which points out that chronology and category do not always run smoothly. In the room with the Poons and Miller paintings hung an example of the 1980s counterfeit abstract art, *Final Sequence* (1987) by Peter Halley. This painting did not belong in this show.

I have written this letter mainly from my memory of the work in the show. It is the *experience* of the show that I wish to convey and some of the thoughts that occurred to me while I viewed it. I bought a copy of the catalogue that day and I have read every word in it. When I write again, I will discuss what I found there. So file this letter, Reader; you may want to refer to it when you read me next time.

1990

Abstraction-Geometry-Painting. The catalogue.

In my last letter, I wrote about the exhibition *Abstraction-Geometry-Painting* at the Albright-Knox Gallery in Buffalo. I promised that this time I would write about the catalogue for that show. The show was organized by Michael Auping, chief curator of the Gallery. The catalogue was published by Abrams, N.Y. in association with the Gallery. The title page reads: *Abstraction-Geometry-Painting: Selected Geometric Abstract Painting in America Since 1945. Organized and with an essay by Michael Auping*. It is a very nice book.

Let me tell you, Reader, what I do with an exhibition catalogue. While the show is fresh in my mind, I look at all the reproductions to check for any that are printed upside-down or sideways and I make pencil notes on those pages. I note any reproductions of works not in the show, and somewhere I will indicate by diagram any work that I saw in the show that is not in the catalogue. I have a respect for books; I don't like to write on their pages, but I know no better way to preserve a catalogue as an accurate reference for a show.

This book was well designed. In the section, "Works in the Exhibit," the paintings are reproduced full-page and in colour. The section, organized by artist, includes a photograph of each artist and a page of text written or spoken in interview by that artist. On the evening of the day I saw the show, I checked the reproductions in the catalogue and I marked (spoiled) five pages of my new book. Later that evening, I found myself thinking about two paintings I had seen in the show and it occurred to me that I had not seen them in the catalogue. I went back to the book; they were not there. An artist was missing from the catalogue! I wracked my brains to recall the artist's name for it was one of those in the show that had been new to me—Michael Loew.[1]

I began to read the catalogue, not with the curator's essay, but with the texts by the artists. For me, these are the most important texts in a catalogue because they give evidence of the artists' thinking. If I am to understand an artist's work, I believe that the artist will help me do so by his choice of words and the thoughts those words address. Artists' statements are sometimes difficult; I read them slowly and thoughtfully. Within a week after seeing the show, I had read all of the artists' texts.

The usual artists' biographies were omitted from this catalogue, and in their place is a section called "Artists' Bibliographies and Selected Exhibitions and Reviews." These lists cover the period from 1945 to 1988. I could not learn, for instance, what Burgoyne Diller or Fritz Glarner had done before 1945. Lists of published writing "by the artist" are short— sometimes only an interview is cited, or nothing is listed as is the case with three of the artists. Lists of published writing "on the artist" together with one-artist shows and cited reviews run to seven columns for Josef Albers and to 10 columns for Kenneth Noland. This is useful information and I was happy to see it given, but I regretted the omission of biographies. Biographies for those artists who were new to me would have immediately informed me; the bibliographies, instead, gave me work to do. I have to look up the sources, and for the artists about whom I wish to learn, the bibliographies are among the shortest in the book. It is clear that the bibliographies, as substitutes for biographies, down-play the artists' histories and give greater prominence to the writing and interpretations of art critics.

The essay by Michael Auping is an ambitious history of the period covered by the exhibit and by current standards it is excellent. (There are 290 footnotes.) The title, "Fields, Planes, Systems: Geometric Abstract Painting in America Since 1945," suggests that Auping was having trouble with words. In his introduction, he discusses nomenclature. One learns that most classifications are supplied by critics ("field" is attributed to Clement Greenberg, and "hard-edge" to Lawrence Alloway), and that many artists find these words inadequate, or they would supply their own definitions of them. In interviews with the artists, Auping tells us, the word "geometry" was unanimously disparaged. One wonders why Auping proceeded with the word. There appear to be two reasons. The first is found in his "Acknowledgements," where he thanks the artists he interviewed and goes on to say: "While their responses were... insightful, they should not be held responsible for my appropriation or transformation of their original ideas." This allowed Auping some liberty with his interpretations. The second reason is that Auping has based his essay on the critical history of the period. He begins with Alfred H. Barr, Jr.

Alfred Barr was the first director of New York's Museum of Modern Art (established in 1927). In 1936, Barr prepared and published a chart called "The Development of Abstract Art." The chart begins with the painters of the 1890s in Paris, and by a complex progression showing cross-references and influences, stops at 1925 with Surrealism in Paris and the Bauhaus in Germany. Then the chart divides into two streams— the one Barr called "non-geometric abstract art" and the other, "geometric abstract art." A synopsis of the chart usually places expressionist abstract art (Kandinsky) on one side, and geometric abstract art (Mondrian) on the other. European modernism is summed up in this way. The chart is an analysis of the development of modernist painting in Europe, and it reflects Barr's knowledge and understanding of it in 1936.

In his essay, Auping adopts Barr's chart and its two streams of abstract art: the expressionistic, intuitional and emotional mode, and the geometrical and intellectual mode. With baggage in each hand, so to speak, Auping proceeds. In 1944, he points out, Mondrian died in New York. (He does not add that Kandinsky died in Paris that same year.) "Geometry" is the word, 1945 is the year, and America is the place.

Auping devoted 10 pages to "Early American Abstraction." I thought these were among the best pages in the essay. The years between the Armory show (1913) and the founding of the American Abstract Artists group (1937) are surveyed, and I found in Auping's tale many of the artists I had hoped to see in the show. Mondrian's years in New York and the admiration of those artists who knew him are told in quotes from artists. Moving along, Auping begins his chapter called "Gesture vs. Geometry: The New York School," and he runs smack into Barnett Newman who stops him dead.

Auping devotes four pages to Newman here, and for the remaining 40 pages of the essay, the reader never loses sight of him. Auping cannot advance without Newman; his work is too important and its effect has been so great that it is impossible to get around him. So Auping goes through him to carry his essay forward, but he could not put Newman's work into the exhibition.

During his lifetime, Barnett Newman refused to have his work associated with "geometric painting." Newman's widow has declined all invitations to include his work in exhibitions under that rubric. Auping quotes from a letter Newman wrote to John Gordon, curator of the Whitney Museum, in 1962 which says in part: "I have given the show you contemplate doing, 'Geometric Abstraction,' a great deal of thought... I realize the point you wish to make but I honestly cannot convince myself that by amalgamating me with those who do not represent it... you can make the point about me... Mine is, I believe, a new kind of painting, devoid of plastic dogmas and totally unrelated... to theirs, [and] the inclusion of my work... would... only confuse the issues. I did not come out of the world they advocate. To make me part of it or to present me as its culmination would... distort my work and my history." I wish more artists had Newman's strength of conviction, his integrity and his courage.

Auping believes that his exhibition addresses the question of "whether *we can speak* of a definable geometric tradition in postwar American abstract art" (italics mine). Indeed, some speak too much. The essay is a compilation of the work and words of those art critics who are known in America as "spokesmen" or "theorists" for artists. Auping surveys the Survey Shows: *Post-Painterly Abstraction* (1964), *Systems Painting* (1966) and *Primary Structures*. He adopts the criteria the curator/critics have laid down, and he draws from these shows those artists' works that best represent them. (Auping chaffs both Greenberg and Alloway for including some artists in their shows whose work does not entirely fit the criteria!) The essay, then, is really about the history of art criticism in America since 1945, and the exhibition was selected to represent it. In light of this, Auping is justified in including in his essay those artists he understands as "critics"— Tim Ebner, Philip Taaffe, Ross

Bleckner, Peter Halley— and in putting Halley's painting in the exhibition. Since 1945, American art critics have usurped the authority of artists and exploited it, and in the 1980s, artists have appropriated and exploited the work of other artists. "Neo-geo" is entrenched now as part of social history however poor it is as art.

You may think, Reader, that I am critic-bashing and Michael Auping is the target. Not so. I was sympathetic with Auping throughout his essay, and I was saddened by it on his behalf. Had Auping seen that Barr's chart was obsolete, he would not have been trapped by it. Had he abandoned the word "geometry," his exhibition might have been a revelation and he could have put Barnett Newman's paintings in it. But Auping chose to follow the interpreters instead of the painters, and he missed the opportunity to explode their myths.

Barr's chart fails precisely because it separates what wants to be joined together. In his attempt to connect one modern "ism" to another, Barr concentrated on *form* as content. It is *colour* that links both streams of abstract art, but it will require a profound understanding of colour and its interrelationship with form to see this. Because it is only theory, Barr's chart must be demolished; *observation* will unite the two streams. Critics have not done this yet; rather, they conserve theory and sacrifice art. Today, a generation of artists have studied the critics' texts instead of the artists' paintings, and now a counterfeit art masquerading as a new criticism is the result.

The word "geometry" separates and misleads; the word that will unite the streams of modernist art is "concrete." This word is found in writings by modernist painters; it denotes perceptual consciousness and it describes both painting and poetry. In painting, "concrete" defines visual phenomena, its reality and its necessity. For years, poets have been using this word. Concrete poetry developed from Hugo Ball (Dada, Zurich 1916), from Alexei Kruchenykh (Zaum, Russia 1913) and from that American in Paris, Gertrude Stein. Poets and painters share the same history of modernist thought and art. De Stijl's Theo van Doesburg published his poems in the Dada journals; Kandinsky and Josef Albers wrote and published poetry. Abstract and non-objective paintings are *concrete painting* and have been since the 1890s. ("Remember that a painting... is essentially a flat surface on which colours have been arranged in a particular order." Maurice Denis, 1890.)

Painters favoured the word "concrete," but it is "geometric" and "geometry" that have been preserved to separate paintings and distort the meaning of art.

1990

Note:

1. There were no reproductions, no photographs or text and no bibliography for Michael Loew and he was not mentioned in the catalogue essay. I wrote to the Gallery for information about this artist. In reply I received a sheet of *Addenda and Errata* which listed six omitted paintings and six others that had been reproduced or described incorrectly. With regard to Michael Loew, I was sent a photocopy of a published commentary on his work with a brief biography. Michael Loew (1907-1985) was an early member of the A.A.A. The paintings in the show were *Shifting Space* (1952) and *Six of a Kind, Nothing Wild* (1979). If you are an artist, Reader, I suggest you think long and hard about this oversight.

Voice of Fire. The controversy.

Now that the dust seems to have settled, I want to review the nation-wide controversy that arose over the National Gallery of Canada's purchase of Barnett Newman's painting, *Voice of Fire.* As with most art stories, the news media favoured absurdity, centred on controversy, and promoted uninformed opinion as the barometer of consensus.

The earliest radio reports focused on the cost of the painting ($1.76 million) and the number of colours in it (two). A statement by a representative of CAR/FAC (Canadian Artists' Representation/le Front des artistes canadiens) was interpreted as a vote against the painting because Newman was not Canadian and all Canadian artists were tarred with the same media-brush. It is to our shame that the most prominent uninformed opinions on the painting came from the Tory MP from Manitoba who was chairman of the House of Commons Culture Committee, Felix Holtmann. The controversy over the Newman painting seems to have run deeper, lasted longer and spread further than most art news stories are made to do.

In June, I visited Ottawa. I had two things on my mind; I would see the painting, *Voice of Fire*, and I would read all the newspaper clippings and radio and television transcripts on the topic of the purchase that were on file at the National Gallery. I had written to Helen Murphy, the assistant director of Communications and Marketing at the Gallery, and she had arranged that the files be made available to me. For five hours, I sat at a desk in an office in the curatorial wing of the National Gallery reading the four thick files of material that had been gathered between March 7th (the day the Gallery released the news of the purchase) and the first week of May. I read clippings from newspapers in Ottawa, Montreal, Toronto, Saskatoon, St. John and Los Angeles, letters to the editor from the major Canadian papers, and articles from *Maclean's* magazine and CCA's (Canadian Conference of the Arts') *Art News.* I read transcripts from news broadcasts on radio and television, interviews with the Gallery's director Shirley Thomson, and curator Brydon Smith, and arts reports and commentaries by Hal Anthony, Doug Small, Robert Enright, Fred Innis and Matt Blair. As I read through this mountain of material, I saw a pattern emerging.

On March 7th and 8th, Ottawa, Montreal and Toronto newspapers carried CP (Canadian Press) reports about the purchase. These were factual reports based on the Gallery's press release and substantiated with additional information from both Shirley Thomson and Brydon Smith. Radio reports on March 7th were condensed to a short item of news. The item, then, was picked up by radio journalists and extended for commentary. These commentaries, often comedic, focused on the point that a painting could not, or should not, cost the greater part of the National Gallery's annual purchasing budget. From the start, the electronic media ignored the facts about the purchase and featured the cost versus the simplicity of the painting. On March 8th, Christopher Hume reported in the *Toronto Star* that Canadian artists (meaning a CAR/FAC spokesperson) were against the work, and on that same day in an interview on CFRB, Shirley Thomson was told that a Toronto artist disapproved of the purchase. When Thomson asked "Who?", the interviewer was unable to answer. Misrepresentation was given media credibility.

You would be surprised, Reader, at the number of interviews the people at the National Gallery had with the media on those first few days and the amount of information that was given in them. But the newspapers had begun to feed on the electronic media, and the facts about the painting and the Gallery's procedure for the purchase were shunted aside. The media took and maintained a naive position of protest against an artist they did not know had existed, a work they had not heard about or seen, and a purchase price that could be made to appear inordinately high in comparison to the National Gallery's meagre budget. Details regarding Newman's life and work, its effect on painting internationally and in Canada, and the significance of *Voice of Fire* to Canadians were beyond their grasp.

On March 9th, the CBC reported that the National Gallery would be called upon to explain the Newman purchase to the House of Commons Culture Committee and this brought Felix Holtmann on-stage. (It could be argued that the media had set the stage for Holtmann; his part would be most vocal, most visible and completely predictable.) Holtmann claimed that he could make the Newman painting with two cans of paint, two rollers and about 10 minutes work. If Holtmann had not been chairman of the Commons Culture Committee, he would have been funny. As it was, his credentials as a pig-farmer were snapped up by the media and we did not learn how he qualified as an authority on art. While Holtmann clowned for the press, a serious matter had surfaced; that is, the right of the curatorial staff at the National Gallery of Canada to make decisions about the purchase of major works for the collection. All of the interviews given by the Gallery's director and curators were as nothing compared to the antics of Holtmann. The Gallery's traditional arm's length from the government in administrative and artistic decisions was under attack.

The story grew. Efforts to sort reality from ridicule were given short shrift. The media were happy with the state of their art. The country was divided into "art critics" who were for the work and a media invention called John Q. Public who was against it. It was not hard to tell the man-on-the-street that $1.76 million was too much of his tax-money to spend on a painting so that in interviews he responded on cue with outrage; it was disturbing, however, to count the number of people in the art community who ran to jump into John Q. Public's shoes— like John Robert Colombo and Charles Pachter. Those who defended the purchase did so with some knowledge of the painting and the artist who made it. There were published statements by Yves Gaucher, Brenda Wallace, Guido Molinari, René Blouin and Avrom Isaacs in support of the purchase, but what these people said was not given wide exposure. Their thoughts were difficult for the media to process and they were not much fun.

The controversy was covered by the *Los Angeles Times* on March 29th. In the article, John Robert Colombo was named as Canada's most prominent art critic and Felix Holtmann, pig-farmer, was Canada's Minister of Culture. Readers in Los Angeles learned that Canada's artists, art critics, the general public and the government were unanimously against the Newman painting and the National Gallery's expenditure of $1.8 million for it. I admit, Reader, that I felt ashamed of Canada when I read this article.

On April 5th, Felix Holtmann was interviewed on CBC's *Morningside*. He was serious news now and his life as a Member of Parliament, a Manitoba pig-farmer and chairman of the Commons Culture Committee was reviewed. *Voice of Fire*, its cost and its simplicity, was also discussed. Holtmann believed he had gotten to the nub of the problem when he said that there had to be more private sector funding and less government funding for the arts. One cannot help but wonder what country Holtmann thinks he is living in. Of course, private sector funding would be preferred and every artist, curator and gallery in the country would endorse it. But Holtmann had just been party to one of the worst charades over art in our history. Having played the role of a mindless agitator against a work of art, how would he bring the Canadian private sector on side to support what he himself had ridiculed? I regret that Peter Gzowski did not have the presence of mind to ask him this, or to ask him if he had read the *Massey Report* or any of the white papers on the status of the artist in Canada that governments have been accumulating for years.

In April, the issue around the painting entered a new phase. Arts journalists began to chastise the people at the National Gallery. In an article in the *Globe and Mail*, Stephen Godfrey advised the Gallery staff that they should have *explained* the painting and made the purchase *understandable* to the public. In Godfrey's view, the Gallery had done everything wrong. Godfrey reported that the National Gallery was about to issue a brochure on the painting written by Brydon Smith. By suggesting that the brochure might be "too little, too late," he effectively undermined this effort by the Gallery even before it appeared.

On April 21st, Bronwyn Drainie, another *Globe and Mail* arts journalist, took aim at *Voice of Fire*, at Barnett Newman and at what she called the painting's "elitist message." Drainie had done some homework, or she may have spoken to someone with post-modern Marxist ideas. She characterized the New York school (abstract expressionism) as arrogant, egotistical and inhuman. She deplored "its baleful influence which continues to this day, especially among artists who don't keep up with the trends." Drainie's short-sighted view of abstract art is both anti-art and anti-intelligent, and with it, she explained why "we, as a society, hate this red and blue striped painting..." Drainie's diatribe would have gladdened the hearts of Adolf Hitler and Joseph Stalin, for it was with her arguments that Germany's modernist artists were routed to America after 1933, and Russia's cultural doors were closed after 1922. I don't believe that Drainie's intention was sinister; rather, her research into art and social history was inadequate. She clearly revealed her motive when she described works by Newman and Rothko— "they glare back at you austerely, just daring you to say something banal." Before these artists' works, Drainie transfers her own sense of failure to the paintings. Drainie supported the National Gallery purchase only because the painting "represents... a once-powerful but spiritually dead-end artistic movement which is, one can only hope, gone forever." Drainie's message is extremely dangerous; it encourages hatred of things one does not understand.

On the morning of April 10th, Shirley Thomson, the National Gallery's director, addressed the House of Commons Culture Committee. I have read the published *Remarks* that she delivered that day. It reviews the fiscal year 1989-90 and projects the Gallery's plans and priorities for 1990-91 with regard to the buildings, the exhibition program, the educational and publishing programs, and collections and acquisitions. *Voice of Fire* is treated as a separate topic and the purchase of the painting is accounted for within the Gallery's mandate. Newspaper reports on Ms. Thomson's defence of the purchase, however, described the 14 assembled MPs with Felix Holtmann at centre wearing a red and blue neck-tie. Holtmann had succeeded not only in ridiculing the painting, but in trivializing government.

On the night of April 10th, CBC's *The Journal* featured the story of the controversy around Newman's *Voice of Fire*. The top interviewee was Felix Holtmann. He restated that the painting was too simple, was by an American and that it was too expensive. After this, it would be uphill all the way; Shirley Thomson was interviewed next to begin the struggle. After Thomson, a brief history of Barnett Newman was done by Paul McGrath; then, Canadian sculptor Robert Murray (who had known Newman) was interviewed from New York. I quote from the transcript:

Murray— One of the difficulties about our easy access to works of art is that

> we've been conditioned by this media [television] in particular to have the attention span of a gopher, and I think the assumption that one is somehow going to be given instant information by confronting a painting is folly. You can only take away from it the kind of understanding that you bring to it, and the experience of the painting.

After a station break, *The Journal* continued with a panel discussion. Ydessa Hendeles and Christopher Hume were presented as defenders of the painting/purchase, and Jane Martin (CAR/FAC) and John Robert Colombo appeared to stand against it. Martin clarified her position when she said that she wanted the National Gallery's purchasing priority to be Canadian art. (Notice, Reader, that the Gallery's priority *is* Canadian art, but art market values in Canada mean that no Canadian modernist painting is valued at $1.76 million.) Colombo pointed out that the National Gallery owned no works by Charles Pachter or Louis de Niverville, two Canadian artists about whom he had written in the past. (The National Gallery owns *Through a Looking Glass* by Louis de Niverville, purchased in 1964.)

The panel discussion was doomed from the start. The members had been chosen, not for their knowledge of Newman and the painting, but as adversaries who had jumped into the fray of a media debate. One wonders if a different panel could have better served the viewers of *The Journal*—one, for instance, which included David Mirvish or John Bentley Mays, Robert Stacey or Roy Kiyooka. As it was, the panel was both led and restrained by the CBC interviewer. When the panelists tried to speak of the importance of Newman's work, they were interrupted with, "We'll get to the aesthetics later," and when the discussion ended, "the aesthetics" had not been addressed at all. This edition of *The Journal* is an example of manipulation. While the CBC may feel justified in focusing on the battle-lines of an existing debate, it did nothing that would contribute to its clarification or resolution. *The Journal* had presented positions of greatest opposition, promoted art as commodity, and characterized the Canadian public as hapless consumers on whom the Newman painting had been foisted.

It would appear that radio, television and even newspapers are poor communication vehicles, or because they address a mass audience, they are extremely limited. In the case of *Voice of Fire*, they were unable to disseminate the most fundamental information about the purchase; to communicate the more subtle aspects of the painting was impossible. I have not dealt here with the T-shirt or the facsimile painting which gave the media a field-day of entertaining opportunities; rather, I have chosen to examine those who characterize themselves, and are acknowledged to be, spokesmen, arts journalists and responsible reporters— in other words, the media elite.

The arm's-length principle had remained an issue. On March 18th, Deputy Prime Minister Don Mazankowski said that an expenditure review committee would try to stop the purchase. The purchase, completed in August, was impossible to undo. On April 27th, Tory MP Larry Schneider put a motion before the Commons Culture Committee to ask the National Gallery to resell Newman's painting. This scenario is ludicrous— here we had a group of politicians adamantly against the expenditure of $1.76 million for a painting they didn't understand. Because they had been assured that the painting had been purchased for less than market value (estimates of its value ranged up to $3 million), they, like greedy opportunists, were busy thinking about reselling the painting for a profit. Fortunately, the committee's vote ran against the motion. However, if pillage won't work, maybe punishment will. As late as June 6th, the press reported that Tory MP Don Blenkarn, chairman of the House of Commons Finance Committee, had filed a motion to block the National Gallery from receiving $1.8 million of its 1990-91 allotment from the government. Barnett Newman should be heard on this matter. I quote from his cultural manifesto written in 1933 when he was 27 years old:

> It is humanity's tragedy that today its leaders are either sullen materialists or maniacs who express the psychopathology of the mob minded.

You may think, Reader, that my view of the events following the National Gallery's purchase of Barnett Newman's *Voice of Fire* is biased. Of course it is. I am a painter; I have a stake in this country, in its culture and its future. I expect government to be genuinely concerned about the cultural life of the country; I expect the media to report information responsibly. Both, in their handling of the purchase of *Voice of Fire*, promoted sensationalism for self-serving ends. For them, visual art is not important enough to be taken seriously, and the opportunity the Newman painting gave them to appeal to the general public and the innocent taxpayer could not be missed. I am a taxpayer, too. Because my knowledge and understanding of this artist and this painting is incomplete, I want our National Gallery to own the painting *for me*. I will take this American-made painting in place of only one of the American-made CF18 jet-fighter planes ($35 million) that the government has purchased for Canada's defence. In years to come, *Voice of Fire* will speak for humanity long after all the CF18s have fallen from the sky.

1990

Voice of Fire. The painting.

In the wake of the controversy following the National Gallery's purchase of Barnett Newman's *Voice of Fire*, I have decided to write about that painting. I am aware that this will be a formidable undertaking because *Voice of Fire* is to be *seen*. It would seem an easy matter to describe the painting's size, its shape and the colours in it; I could give details about its history and the history of the artist, or I could review the climate of the 1960s art world when American abstract expressionist painting was prominent. But I prefer to write about the painting as a visual event. I want to speak of it in the same way Newman spoke of his and other artists' paintings when he wrote:

> The image we produce is the self-evident one of revelation, real and concrete, that can be understood by anyone who will look at it without the nostalgic glasses of history.[1]

To begin, I want to say something about seeing and thinking, and about what one sees and what one says about what one sees. In psychology, recept (sensation), percept and concept are understood to be a progressive, accumulative action of the mind. This action culminates in the formation of a classifying language. The concept (word) is said to be the pinnacle of an experience, and sensation and perception are mere steps toward that goal. The psychologist concludes, then, that *thought* is achieved with the formation of a concept. When we see, we say what we see (talk), and what we say is proof of our seeing.

To write about seeing I will use words. But seeing is perception, and words are concepts. For a painter, *seeing is thinking*; it is a non-verbal form of thought. However difficult it is to describe the experience of visual perception, I believe that it is by this means, and this means alone, that people respond to paintings. The eye receives light (recept), the mind is engaged (percept), and the emotions are aroused. In this way, people see a painting, they know that they are seeing it, and they respond or react to it. I suggest that the concept (word), when it is formulated, is an analogue for the experience which resides in the action of sensation and perception, and that it articulates, not the experience of the present, but a similar experience recalled from another time. This accounts for the words (talk) that follow the experience of perception. The observer has opened a file of like-experience stored in the mind to which words have already been assigned.

People accept the authority of words, but they seem less able to grasp the authenticity of what they see. They *name* what they see, fix it within the context of a previous experience, and only then will they say that it has meaning. In doing this, people are fixing what is present into their pasts, and some will even regard themselves to be the authors of what they see. This accounts for a lot of art criticism. It is why some people don't like a painting if it does not conform to something they have seen before; it explains how some people who have looked at *Voice of Fire* say that it is nothing.

If that which strikes the eye (sensation) and mind (perception) is not noticed *consciously*, the observer, incited by his vision, will fix upon a pretext with which he will name the experience. Such an observer has not grasped what is present and real; rather, he has interrupted his seeing and turned his mind inward in search of preconceptions to represent what is present. This inward search is not authentic; it interferes with the seeing and it constitutes what Newman called "the nostalgic glasses of history."

Throughout the 1980s, trends in painting have been toward representation. This art satisfies those who like to name what they see, or identify it with something they have seen before. The viewer can understand the painting immediately if he has already seen its topic on television or read about it in a newspaper. Sometimes, the viewer is confounded by the painting because he is unable to determine whether the artist is in support of, or against, the issue addressed. This art examines social and moral values. Since the 1970s, conceptual art has also addressed values. It is a critical art and it gives the viewer much to weigh and measure in his mind. It begs for a conclusion from the viewer. It shows itself (see this?); it questions (what do you think?), and the viewer responds to it in this way. Art that does not represent, does not address issues, does not question, is called "high art" and it was given this name in the 1960s. It is in this category that Barnett Newman's paintings have been placed.

The words "high art" suggest an exclusiveness that offends many people. This is unfortunate because what has been called high art is often an art of revelation. Newman said that his work "can be understood by anyone who will look..." Surely, this is not exclusive, but intends to be inclusive of everyone. Among artists, there is a strong consciousness of fundamental *human* experience. That Newman understood his own humanity is communicated in his work and his paintings appeal to the humanity of the viewer. They do this when the viewer acknowledges what is real and present, and if he can be said to recognize something in that acknowledgement, it is his own capacity for intelligence. Newman's is an intelligent art; it is "revelation, real and concrete." I would call Newman's art *concrete painting*.

What does the observer see when he looks at *Voice of Fire*? The painting is *self-evident*; it is a particular size, a particular shape, it is divided in a particular direction by two particular colours. This did not occur by accident; rather, Newman made it this way deliberately. It is the size, the shape, the direction and the colour that I will write about here. These things are real and concrete.

The painting is large. It is 18 feet high and eight feet wide. That is three times the height of a man and wider than his arm span. The viewer is "surrounded" by the size of the painting when he is standing close to it and all of it is within his field of vision. The nearer the observer is to the painting, the more he may feel himself enveloped by it. The dimensions of the work are awesome, not because the viewer feels small before it, but because he sees the painting's magnitude.

The painting's vertical shape is separated vertically (twice) to give the surface three equal vertical areas. This insistence of verticality and of equivalence in the painting confirms the boundary of the work. Because the painting is 18 feet high, each shape is 18 feet high. The viewer, standing before the painting, encounters an image which "stands" before him.

There are two colours in the painting. One occupies the vertical shape at the centre of the painting— it is called "red"; the other occupies the two vertical shapes on each side of the centre shape— it is called "blue." Each shape is a dense solid surface of colour. When standing close to the work, one can see the faint strokes of application. The painting cannot be called impersonal; rather, these marks are subtle evidence of Newman's person making this work and they speak of his presence in it. I think it is fair to describe the work as simple. It has been said that less is more, and not to confound you, Reader, I will tell you what more is in this painting.

If there is a question to be asked by the viewer, it is "What is happening here?" and what one consciously sees at work is the answer to that question. The "red" in the painting is a cadmium red pigment; the "blue" is ultramarine blue. These colours have been applied pure (unmixed). Cadmium red is an opaque pigment and ultramarine is transparent, whether they are in the tube, on the palette, or applied to a canvas. Newman has set the qualities of these two pigments to work in *Voice of Fire*. The red, dense, intense and opaque, reflects the greater amount of light to the viewer's eye. The blue, darker, absorbs light, but due to its transparent quality, light passes through it and is reflected from the white ground to the viewer's eye. The pairing of this opaque red and this transparent blue creates a contrast of hue and substance; the capacity of each colour to reflect so much light, each in a different way, brings about an equivalence of the two colours. But there is more.

This red (cadmium) carries in it qualities of yellow. That means that both red and yellow light are reflected from its surface. This blue (ultramarine) carries in it qualities of red. That means that both blue and red light pass through it and are reflected from the white ground. This combination of colours, then, is able to behave in extraordinary ways and anyone (everyone) can see it. The red shape at centre, abutted by the blue shapes at each side, is both red and red-orange; the blue shapes are both cool and warm, blue and purple. Let the viewer's eye absorb all of the light of the red, and the blue will darken; let the eye absorb the transparent dark of the blue, and the red will burn to orange. Red/blue, blue/orange, purple— the painting is on fire; like a great lick of flame, the red flows upward at its centre. Newman called it *Voice of Fire* and he believed everyone would be able to see its primal energy and understand the universality of its particular event. All of this is real and concrete and visible.

By using words, I have had to describe separately the elements of size, shape, direction and colour. My words will read like an analysis, but the painting is a synthesis. All of the things that I have written about separately are perceived together as *one thing* at once and may be seen in a moment. That moment is sustained; the painting endures. What is seen is not a trick of the eye; rather, it is a phenomenon revealed, achieved by Newman at the height of his creativity. Barnett Newman is dead, but this work endures and gives to viewers what Newman called "an experienced moment of total reality." There is no need to search for symbolism here— the painting presents; it does not represent. Each time the viewer returns to see it, it begins for him again. It is the viewer who comes to and goes from the work; the painting, unchanged, endures. If the viewer has not been open to seeing the painting, perhaps his time will come. Art waits for its audience.

How, then, does one respond to the phenomenon of the work and the experience of one's seeing? Each person responds differently from each other, but for Newman, it is known that when he saw what he had made he spoke of "exaltation." He called it "the sublime" in art. These words are considered passé now and most people will not use them; they recall too quickly that exclusiveness that so offends them. Newman used these words to express a profound human experience. He did not regard himself to be higher in mind than others, but one with humanity. If, on seeing *Voice of Fire*, we want to search our past for its meaning, then we must search deep into the experience of mankind for that primordial human response that must have occurred when man, in the dawn of consciousness, first saw the sun, knew that he was seeing it, and was filled with wonder by it.

1991

Note:

1. Barnett Newman. "The Sublime is Now." *Tiger's Eye 1* (15 December 1948).

The Myth of the Artist's Five-Year Career.

There is a myth about artists that has been floating around for the past 20 years. It says that, in Canada, an artist's career is about five years long. This is a generalization, of course, but it is meant to be. Some artists' careers last ten years and some enjoy "fame" for two or three years only. Others whose reputations are impressed on the mind of the art-viewing public become "names," and their careers are sustained even when their work is not visible. We can all think of an artist whose name brings an image to mind, but whose work we have not seen for a long time.

I remember a conversation on this topic that I had with the sculptor Robert Downing almost 20 years ago. At that time, only a few Canadian artists could be described as having "made it." I ventured that the Canadian art public seemed unable to sustain more than six or seven artists as "stars" at any one time. Robert agreed; he had experienced considerable success and was aware of the fickleness of the Canadian art world. Since then, the population of artists has grown. Over the past 10 years, the number of artists whose work is visible has increased tremendously. However, only recently in conversation with an art critic, I had to defend certain artists whose work had not been seen lately. This art critic had commented that artists were unreliable because so many of them quit working after a short time. I knew that the artists in question were still working; their work simply was not being shown and I said so. I was reminded of the myth of the artist's five-year career and I intend in this letter to examine it.

For artists, making art is a life-long commitment. As students in art, artists determine the strength of their will and the scope of their vision. Some will pursue, others will abandon, a life of making art. Once committed, the artist will give priority to his work over all other preoccupations. Many artists can work in their studios without concern for a show-place or an audience, but eventually, they will want to share what they have made with other people. There are artists whose work depends on place and audience— they are the installation and performance artists. All this does not describe the artist's career; it defines the artist's life. A career occurs *outside* the artist's studio, not in it, and it is directly dependent on a dealer, and on curators and critics. I believe that it is from these people that the myth of the artist's five-year career has arisen.

Ideally, dealers, curators and critics are people whose interest in art is impassioned, objective and informed. Each plays an important role in making art visible and accessible to the art-viewing public. The dealer offers a show-place; the curator who is attached to a collecting institution offers custodianship for art and access to it to scholars and students; the critic, whether an art reporter or a critical historian, takes on the task of documenting and classifying art for a general or select public and for future generations. Each has a heavy responsibility because eventually all artists are dependent on them for their survival and for the survival of their work.

In the past 20 years, the number of dealers, curators and critics has grown. Those students in art who did not pursue a life of making art sometimes used their knowledge in these areas. More recently, arts studies in universities have created greater numbers of graduates who have entered these fields. It must be acknowledged that there is a very small audience for art in this country, and that dealers, curators and critics number among that audience along with art students, artists and collectors. The art community, then, is an insular group. It is the collector, both the individual collector and the collecting institution, in whom the dealer has the greatest interest. The curator is interested in the art that the dealer as well as the collector selects; by a direct purchase from a dealer or by a collector's donation, art enters an institution and is made visible to the greater public. The critic is interested in the art shown in private and public galleries, the art purchased for private and public collections, and he gains his authority by his assessment of it. The interrelationship between dealers, curators and critics constitutes a system in which an artist's career is established. But the dealer, curator and critic are also establishing their own careers, and herein lies the source of the myth that an artist's career is only five years long.

A dealer selects the art he wants to exhibit. He promotes the artists he chooses and the artists' works are shown to greatest advantage in the dealer's gallery. By an exhibition in a privately owned gallery (even if no works are sold), an artist's career is begun. Of all the artists working at any given time, only those whose works are chosen for dealers' exhibitions are visible to the art-viewing public. Other artists have little opportunity to find an audience for their work.

Operating a private gallery is a risky business. When galleries open up and close down, artists appear to come and go. Sometimes a dealer will relocate his gallery and will clear the gallery of all the "old" artists and take on "new" ones to give the gallery a new image. Most galleries, even those that are well-established, have a long roster of "past" artists whose work has been shown in their galleries for varying periods of time. In the 1960s and 1970s, an artist was deemed to be responsible if the relationship between artist and dealer failed; it was damaging to the artist's reputation if he left a gallery. Times have changed in this regard. Now, not only do artists move from dealer to dealer (they are free agents), but dealers take on artists to try them out, keep them, or toss them. Of course, some dealers have shown certain artists regularly for the entire life of their galleries, but there are others who have opened and closed business, reopened or relocated, leaving a spew of artists standing on the street.

Recently, owners of private galleries have become predominantly concerned about their galleries' image. This image is the collective impression created by all of the artists' works in the gallery taken together. The gallery, then, is believed to have a life of its own and the artists' works contribute to it. Unfortunately, the artists are interchangeable or dispensable; they can be replaced whenever the dealer wishes to change the gallery's image. In this circumstance, it is the dealer who is the "star" and the gallery as place has primary importance. Where once art gave meaning to a gallery, the dealer's name now lends significance to the art. Such a gallery is called "high-profile," and by reflection, the artists in the gallery are called "high-profile," too. High-profile galleries compete with each other to achieve the greatest prominence. While the struggle for importance among dealers who wish to be regarded as the most advanced is ongoing, it is subject to some major change about every five years.

The traditional domain of the curator is the public gallery. Public galleries can be classified as the small, the medium and the large institutions. Artists must be aware of the people who hold curatorial positions in all of these galleries. They can introduce their work to curators by sending them slides. This practice was begun in the early 1970s when reproductions of art on colour slides were deemed a useful means of initial viewing. In those years, an artist sent slides of his work to the largest galleries, then worked his way down to the smaller ones. The artist's motive was chiefly to make his work known to people who most obviously would be interested in seeing it. Since then, more public galleries have been established and the practice among artists has changed. Now, artists send slides to the smaller galleries requesting an exhibition (an artist may begin his exhibiting career this way), and then work their way upward to the largest galleries.

Curators are career-conscious people who also want to work their way upward from smaller to larger galleries. With the increase of arts graduates from universities, there are more and more people climbing the curatorial ladder. Curators change position regularly; they make in-gallery moves or they move to other galleries. Artists who want to make contact with curators by sending slides know what can happen when a curator's position falls vacant in a gallery. Sometimes the position is left vacant for a prolonged period and artists cannot present their work— there is no one to address. An acting curator may be assigned the position temporarily, but usually this person makes few decisions because the vacating curator has established a program which may be advanced by two or three years. Sometimes the vacated position is considered to be a plum, and all the curators in lesser positions apply for it. Hopeful of getting the position, they neglect their own jobs because they don't expect to be at them much longer. When the coveted job is filled, another position is likely to have come open (the job the new curator has just left), and another scramble to fill that one begins. The changing of curators' positions can accelerate until all the curators seem to be on the move, changing one after another to different positions in different galleries. For artists who are dependent on these people, there is nothing to do but wait and watch. Some artists call this game "musical chairs," and it seems to occur about every five years.

By now, Reader, I suspect you are on to me. You can see that I have taken the myth of the artist's five-year career and applied it to dealers and curators. What I have said is true, but it is a generalization; in other words, the myth is still a myth wherever I put it. To quote bpNichol: "A myth is simply a lie that works."

To complete this thesis, I should apply the myth to the career of the critic, but that is much harder to do. In Canada, not only do we believe that *anyone* can be an artist, but we also allow *everyone* to be a critic. Even intelligent people believe that art is the natural outcome of creative effort, and that *opinion*, however groundless, constitutes criticism. This has made an "artist" of every school child on Friday afternoon and a "critic" of everyone else every day of the week.

Critics are not subject to a five-year career; they can go on indefinitely. Their credibility as critics is enhanced, not by their knowledge of art, but by whatever credentials they have in other fields. Few critics study art; they study other disciplines and apply them to art. A critic needs only one asset—he must be able to write.

Journalism of all stripes is a common training ground for critics. In the past, newspaper columnists from the social page, even from the financial pages, have graduated to the entertainment pages where they became "art critic." (I'm not making this up.) Art magazines which used to publish reviews of art exhibitions now favour articles that examine art in terms of psychology, sociology or literary philosophy. These articles show little knowledge of art or a consciousness of its meaning. In them, art is a metaphor for social, political and psychological behaviour, and the writers examine the commonness of it. That art is *uncommon* has not penetrated the minds of these eager scholars.

Compare the art critic to the literary critic. In the newspapers, most of the book reviews are written by other writers: fiction is reviewed by writers of fiction; poetry is reviewed by poets. In the literary journals, the best criticism is written by critics who are also writers. For instance, read the essays of Louis Dudek, Frank Davey, Stephen Scobie or Douglas Barbour—all are poets. Writers write and they read, and they become skilled at formulating their thoughts and making judgements about what they have read, and they write down their thoughts and judgements *clearly*. Artists, on the other hand, rarely develop writing skills; they often dislike reading. The visual artist is engaged by his perception; it is the stuff of thought. When an artist writes about that thought, he must do a careful job of *translation* from percept (seeing) to concept (words). This is difficult, not impossible, but it is not encouraged. Dealers, curators and critics don't like artists who have too much to say about art. They prefer a submissive artist who will agree with all interpretations of art, even when it is his own work that is under discussion. As a result, artists are considered to be naive, a relatively mindless and inarticulate bunch. Their best asset is their *mysterious* capacity to be creative in spite of themselves. In this atmosphere, artists themselves are leaving the field of art criticism open for any and all takers.

In an art world where writing has greater authority than visual perception, art critics emerge from all quarters. After achieving prominence, some critics go on to become *artists*! Their art is often technically dependent (photography, video, xerox), but occasionally one becomes a painter or a sculptor. A critic who becomes an artist has a better chance for a successful career than an artist who has made a life-long commitment for the same simple reason that Winston Churchill and Tony Curtis are *also* known for their paintings. But then, oh then, Reader, the critic will become the subject of that myth that says that his career will only be five years long.

What is at stake for the artist whose work is a life-long commitment? Why, nothing at all. If he is lucky, he may fit into some high-profile gallery— for a while. He may be championed by some art critic— for a while. He may win curatorial attention even in the largest galleries and his works will be shown and collected by them— for a while. But if luck is not with him, he will have none of this in measure. No matter; he or she will work on and make art for as long as there is life in which to do it.

The artist's five-year career is a myth. It was invented by those who perpetuate it, who trade on it and who even may become entrapped by it. For the artist who is committed to a lifetime of work, it is mouthwash.

1991

Reviews and Articles (1979-1992)

Nancy Davidson's *Untitled: To Margaret Mead.*

Nancy Davidson's work, *Untitled: To Margaret Mead,* is on exhibit at the Art Gallery of Ontario in the exhibition *Four Painters: Joy Walker, Robert McNealy, Peter Hill, Nancy Davidson*.

Davidson's work is an installation, a single work involving one wall of the exhibition space. The work is executed on pieces of paper; the paper is attached directly to the wall. The various paper segments have been brought together to form a two-armed image. The left arm proceeds from the top corner of the wall toward the centre of the wall. The right arm begins at mid-point of the wall's free edge (there is no corner here) and reaches to the wall's centre. The two arms do not meet, but point to each other creating a highly energized space between them. The two shapes "embrace" the wall, measure it, integrating the whole wall— left to right, ceiling to floor— as active image.

It is Davidson's intent to work with "real space." She accepts the wall's space, its measurements as given, and acts upon that space to confirm what she calls, "the wall's autonomy." Her work addresses the wall, activates it, and brings a new measure to it.

The exhibition catalogue reproduces a detail of a working drawing that predates the wall work by about two months. By comparing the drawing to the completed installation, we see something of the development of the work. The drawing shows the artist working in an orderly manner; in it, the two arms of the image are placed almost symmetrically on the page, and the segments, equal in size and shape, combine in pairs in inverted order, creating a near/far relationship which gives an illusion of depth. The drawing's image appears to penetrate the space of the page as well as cross it. In the completed installation, Davidson has successfully eliminated the illusion of depth by interrupting the order of the segments of the work. The illusion of depth was not desirable, for the artist says of her works, "… they do not function as windows to imaginary worlds." Davidson intends to make an immediate statement by the action of the image and its consequence. She says of her works: "They create confrontations in public spaces."

It is of interest to know how the work was made. First, a point about the working drawing reproduced in the catalogue: it is crayon on vellum and the crayon was applied to each paper segment after a piece of corrugated cardboard was placed under the paper. The cardboard was shifted for each segment changing the direction of the pattern. As well, Davidson changed the direction of her stroke. The work is a rubbing, and the procedure is important to the image and to Davidson's concept of the work. Not only is space a given measure, but in the process of developing the work, the pattern of Davidson's image is partly given, or found.

In the wall work, Davidson rubbed the pattern from a concrete floor to create surface on each paper segment. For Davidson, the floor "… contains its own history." The random pattern of the floor, when repeated and collected, reveals its own order. Davidson's sense of the historicity of the commonplace surface of a concrete floor is reflected in the immediacy, or presence, in her work.

The wall work was made with acrylic paint and oil stick on paper. First, each segment was covered with orange acrylic paint; then, each was laid on the concrete floor and a rubbing of the floor was made with a red oil stick. The red, applied over the orange paint, gives a rich dark reading of that colour. Next, because each segment had begun to show its own structure, Davidson knew she had choices and she made decisions about the placement of the final colour. She says that she worked intuitively in response to the image so far evolved. Before the final colour, green, was added, white paint was applied to undercoat it and to conserve its opacity. This was done randomly and rhythmically; spots of white were applied to be painted green later. When the green acrylic was applied, Davidson's stroke sometimes overshot the white undercoat. Where this occurs, the green, transparent over the red or orange, appears to be black; this adds a textured appearance on close inspection.

Davidson says that throughout the process of making the work, she was watching it, watching its changes, its development. When the segments of the work were complete and brought to the wall for installation, Davidson still had options open to her. An installation is completed in the act of installing it; this work, as we see it installed, is Davidson's final choice. All other options have been eliminated. The colour collection, greater or lesser green activity, more or less red activity— these choices were made by Davidson as she attached the pieces to the wall. The working drawing shows the development of the work; the installation *is* the work.

This installation is dedicated to Margaret Mead. Davidson's words best express her reason for this tribute. "It is the *energy* of Margaret Mead, the *energy* of that woman that I wanted to express through the *energy* of the piece." Margaret Mead, anthropologist and social activist, died in 1978. Davidson's work developing this piece occupied her for the greater part of that year. The work is about a life, but it is also about that life ending. Davidson's installation is dependent on the wall. When the exhibition ends, the work will come down; without the wall it has no existence. For those of us who have seen it, it can exist only in our memories.

1979

The Canada Council Art Bank Exhibition at I.G.A. Gallery, Toronto.

The Canada Council Art Bank purchases the work of Canadian artists and rents it to government departments and agencies. Last year, Art Bank opened an Exhibition Gallery and Visual Arts Resource Centre at 2279 Gladwin Crescent in Ottawa. The exhibition at Toronto's I.G.A. Gallery is another step in bringing the works in the Art Bank Collection to the public at large.

This year is the 25th anniversary of the Canada Council. It is also the 10th year of Art Bank's operation. About 10,000 works of art have been purchased over that time. Compared to other collections of Canadian art (for instance, the collections in public galleries across the country), the Art Bank's collection is truly representative of Canada's art of the past decade. This exhibition gave viewers the opportunity to see the work that artists have made and the art community has endorsed over the decade. Unlike other Art Bank exhibitions, this show was not curated— the works were chosen because they were available; that is, they were free from rental contracts at the time the exhibition was being arranged.

Art Bank has been purchasing since 1972, but the works purchased sometimes predate the 1970s. That is the case with Roy Kiyooka's *Chevron* (1964) in this exhibition. The chevron of the title is, in fact, two chevrons which enter the canvas from the top and bottom, meeting at the centre. The title and image recall Kenneth Noland's work, but Kiyooka's chevrons are framed by two elliptical shapes. These shapes have become part of Kiyooka's signature. This painting was purchased in 1973. This and other works of the 1960s remind viewers that the Art Bank collection is a repository by consent of artists and jurors, and the works represent the movements, ideas and attitudes of their time. Kiyooka, for instance, has moved on to work in other media; his *Chevron* has become history.

Untitled #3 (1975) by Royden Rabinowitch, a sculpture in cold rolled steel, is 16 inches wide and nine and a half feet long. It rises only three inches from the floor at its highest point. The overlaid geometric shapes on this blade-like sculpture have a refinement that contradicts its obvious weight. The energy involved in the work's contact with the floor is crucial and is one of its formal aspects.

Formal concerns were the subject of many of the works in the exhibition, but the greater number of works were about ideas. Richard Bonderenko's painting, *#3 Green/Purple Heart* (1972), acrylic on canvas, has a green field on which a purple heart and a black triangle lie at centre flanked by two small heart shapes, one red, the other yellow. This is a colour painting; it answers directly and unself-consciously a question of secondary contrast which is emphasized by the primary and complementary colours of the small hearts. Colour accounts for the success of this work, but the symbolic heart shapes suggest that colour is not its subject.

Diana Dean's *Listening to the Birds* (1977), oil on canvas, is a figurative painting. It shows a girl resting on a hillside by a tree in which decorative birds have been painted. Colours are dark in the foreground except for the trunk of a sapling to the left and above the girl. The work is idealized and poetic in spite of the awkward composition and murky colours.

Pierre Ayot's *La Chaise Jaune* (1979) is a photo-silkscreen which hangs on the wall with a chair whose back abuts the frame. A portion of the chair's back has been cut away and the silkscreen image completes the missing part— a witty comment on matter and illusion.

Jacques Hurtubise's electric sculpture, *Eloise* (1969), was installed close to the Ayot work. The viewing space was confined and one was intimately involved with the work. The sculpture combines neon lights and coloured light bulbs that flash yellow, blue and green, and the pattern of the lights is reminiscent of Op Art. The "10 WATTS" stamped on each bulb is a distraction at close quarters. There are more complex electrical systems than this one by Hurtubise, but because of its simplicity and directness, this work is particularly successful.

Sylvia Charney's *Tabernacle* (1979) is a serene work, a wall sculpture made with gesso and oil pastel on masonite. *Tarpaulin Six* (1975) by Betty Goodwin was hung near the Charney piece. Both works have an earthy quality in their colour and texture. They defy the conventions of both sculpture and painting, being neither and both at the same time.

Serge Tousignant's *Géométrisation Solaire Carré 30 Variations* (1979) is a series of photographs showing a square described by the shadows cast by four sticks speared into sand in sunlight. Variations 1-13 were in this exhibition. This work is a fine example of seriality, of sequence and order in nature, in geometry and in photography.

Denis Rousseau's *Un Siècle de Portrait* (1980) consists of four photographs which hang on the wall and a nearby stand which supports a portrait (the subject of the photographs). Of even greater complexity is a work by Mary Janitch, *Cake Box and Dressings* (1973). Janitch's work consists of a cheesecloth "dress" which hangs on a wooden bar suspended from the ceiling in front of 15 black and white photographs. Nearby are three flattened cake boxes on which eight small oil paintings on paper have been mounted. The Rousseau and Janitch works define a problem for the Art Bank and its clients— their multiple parts and unconventional materials make installation difficult. However, it is important that they are in the collection because they represent the move by artists to conceptual art over the past decade. They are *objects* that give new definition to the art object.

The Art Bank collects art objects. By their nature, the performance art of the 1970s and the more esoteric forms of conceptual art are not collectable. This exhibition, viewed as a retrospect of the decade, lacked whole areas of artistic concerns. But the effect of such work has been felt. Art liberates art and art liberates people. I was told that in the Art Bank's 10 years of rentals, sculpture has moved from "difficult to rent" to "popular and desirable." The program is giving its clients an opportunity to exercise their taste and judgement, and they have become more imaginative in their choices.

Works on paper fulfill the conventional idea of an art object, and at the Art Bank they are most sought for rental. In this exhibition there were a large number of works on paper, hung or available for viewing on request. Photographs by Robert Walker, Robert Bourdeau and Alvin Comiter could be seen along with those by Sam Tata, Tim Porter and John Taylor. Through the 1970s, the photograph has become a print alongside the traditional processes of printmaking and it has influenced the printmaker's craft. This influence can be seen in the photo-etching by Hélène Blouin, the photo-silkscreens by Judy Gouin and Michel Leclaire, the photographic print collage by Bradley Struble and the stereoscopic silver prints with viewers by Michael Sowdon.

The traditional printmaking processes were well represented. There were etchings: *Abandoned Ancestors on Bogg's Island* (1971) by David Blackwood, and *La Sieste* by Carl Daoust. Represented by their lithographs were Roger Savage, Richard Sewell, Alan Wood and Douglas Bentham. The silkscreen print is the painter's medium, and the screen prints by Jack Bush, Ken Danby, Rita Letendre, Christopher Pratt, Brian Fisher and John Howlin are as diverse as are these artists' paintings. Denis Forcier's six prints from *Album Quelques-Unes* bring seriality to the process; the directness and flexibility of the medium is seen in prints by Robert Wolfe, Donald Proch and Barbara Hall.

Works on paper include watercolours, and drawings using graphite, coloured pencil, ink or mixed media. There were watercolours by Claude Breeze, Paterson Ewen, and Jerry Grey; drawings by Lenni Workman, Garry Zeweniuk, Roland Poulin, Al McWilliams, Jan Menses, Georganna Malloff, Ernest Lindner, Ann Kipling, Harry Havey and Carol Fraser.

This exhibition was worth mounting and worth seeing. It showed something of what Canada's artists have been doing over the past decade. Despite all of the statistics that surround the Art Bank program and all of the pages of print that describe its purpose and effectiveness, its meaning and the core of its existence is in the individual works that make up the collection.

1982

Vera Frenkel's
In Search Of The True Blue Romance.

Vera Frenkel's installation, *In Search Of The True Blue Romance*, was open for viewing at ARC (Artculture Resource Centre) in Toronto from March 15th to April 4th of this year. The work consisted of a written text titled *Stranger In A Strange Land*, a set, and a videotape titled *Stories From The Front (And The Back): A True Blue Romance*. The gallery was entirely given to the installation which considerably enhanced the work. One could enter the work without distraction or interference from other works (as in a group show), or from other Frenkel pieces (as has occurred in some exhibitions where several of Frenkel's sets have been installed and tapes have been played simultaneously).

Frenkel's works are literary in nature and this work was not an exception. The installation was a narrative, a biography or autobiography that began with Frenkel, proceeded to her videotaped storytellers, and ended with her audience. All contributed to Frenkel's story and she used everything. Frenkel was playing with fiction and fact, and she manipulated the viewer by confronting him.

In an earlier work called *Her Room In Paris* (1979), Frenkel presented as fact the fictional life of Cornelia Lumsden, expatriot Canadian writer. Frenkel played the role of Lumsden in the video; Lumsden was, and has remained, Frenkel's alter-ego— the artist-in-exile. Frenkel's idea that the artist in Canada is an exile in his own country is an ongoing theme in her work. In *Stories From The Front...* Frenkel and 11 storytellers played the exile roles. With Lumsden, fiction became fact; with *Stories*, Frenkel presented fact as fiction. She tried to dissuade the viewer from accepting the documentary truth of the 11 stories on the videotape to achieve a fiction of the whole. The whole installation was Frenkel's fiction and it became a fact of experience for the viewer.

The viewer's credulity was claimed by literary and visual devices and thereby Frenkel achieved authority. The viewer was not informed by the work; rather, he informed it by participating in its commonplace elements. The word "romance" was well chosen for this work. Frenkel's romantic view of herself as artist-in-exile engaged the viewer's sympathy, and together, artist and viewer played out their mutual exile-roles.

The written text was vital to the work. Its enlarged pages were mounted on a wall near the entrance of the gallery. In the text, Frenkel obliquely describes her intention and anticipates the viewer's reaction to the tape. She presents her thesis that the artist is outlawed by society, and in the last section of the text, she prepares the viewer for a futuristic experience. By the time the viewer entered the set and viewed the tape, he had been told that this art he was about to see was the last art in existence, that like the artist, art had been outlawed, too. However, I saw few viewers read the text before viewing the tape, and some didn't read it at all.

Frenkel started her narrative several times in as many different ways. Her choice of words and word-images led to the set and were repeated in the videotape. She fragmented the thread of each developing story, and by using puns, she led the viewer into every cul-de-sac of consciousness. The narrative progressed laterally and depth was sacrificed. The viewer was involved in an adventure, not a profound experience.

The set imitated the text and the video. It included an overstuffed chair and a table with some fruit on it ("the fruit of my experience"). There were book shelves with books that were chosen, not for their content, but for the words in their titles. A mask, a wheel and a hat were objects as well as symbols, for they recurred in both the text and the videotape. In front of the video monitor were four rows of theatre seats for viewers. On the tape, each storyteller sat alone on one of a row of identical seats to tell his story. The viewer facing the monitor was in a position parallel to the storytellers; he physically became part of Frenkel's installation, and eventually, psychologically.

The video gave the viewer 12 interwoven stories told by Frenkel and 11 people who were connected with Vancouver's Western Front. (They are: Jane Ellison, Christa Haukedal, Donna Balma, Patrick Ready, Sylvia

Scott, Elizabeth Chitty, Anna Banana, Avis Rosenberg, Charles Rea, Hugh Poole and Corry Wyngaarden.) It became clear that each person had previously told a story or given a personal account to Frenkel in some intimate situation— over lunch, over dinner or during a drive. Frenkel asked each person to retell his story for her camera. On the tape, the viewer watched them strain for continuity while retelling an experience, an anecdote or a confidence. Frenkel had fragmented these stories and interwoven them with her own. The stories were inconsequential, but the storytellers, co-operating with Frenkel, the understanding exile, showed that they were exiles, too, and the viewer's sympathies were aroused.

In her narrative, Frenkel told the viewer that the storytellers were not the real people from Western Front, but were actors playing their parts. This was a near-fact because each person became an actor for Frenkel's camera. But the camera showed this fiction to be a lie— these were the real people, and they were bad actors. They made self-conscious efforts to be entertaining; they showed their embarrassment and sometimes their pain in exposing personal experiences told to Frenkel in private, now, for the camera's eye. For this reason, Frenkel's fiction failed, as it was intended to fail; the viewer was not transported by the romance because the actors were as real as he was. The video was confounding and Frenkel's story, the twelfth, did not control the fiction she was, or was not, attempting to create. The viewer, as part of the installation, was not addressed by Frenkel, the narrator; rather, he was exploited by her. Not only did he participate, but he also shared responsibility.

Frenkel had to deal with real time in this installation. The video was 62 minutes long; to see the entire installation, about 90 minutes would be required. To overcome the need for sequential viewing, Frenkel used a number of devices to engage the viewer: the reminiscent quality of the set; the fragmented stories and the frequent new starts; the use of puns and symbolism. All served as beginnings for the errant viewer— he could start anywhere.

This multi-media work was potent with nostalgia. The viewer's relationship with the 11 storytellers throughout the video and his own sense of exile isolated him inside Frenkel's fiction. The viewer may not have believed her story, but he experienced it, and that is Frenkel's art. Ultimately, one accepted the whole experience as the *true story*. This story began when the viewer entered the installation and ended when he departed.

1982

8 ARTPARK Projects.

This exhibition at ARC in Toronto, presented eight projects from ARTPARK in Lewiston, New York, that had been made during the summer of 1983. Initiated and curated by Toronto artist Miho Sawada and installed by architect Ted Shore, the exhibition used photo-documentation for the large-scale outdoor works, included some drawings, and in the case of two of the artists, small installation pieces.

Sawada chose eight artists from the 19 who had participated at ARTPARK. She sought common concerns in their works using three criteria: that the artwork address the problem of society by functioning as architecture or furniture apart from traditions; that it be made by hand; that it involve viewer participation. The artists in the exhibition were: Vito Acconci, Robert Booth, Jeffrey Brosk, Scott Burton, Jay Coogan, Richard Kelly, Miho Sawada and Kit-Yin Snyder.

The photo-documentation gave a broad view of each artist's work. Photographs of the works in progress showed them being made and being installed. Photographs of the completed works, however, did not always satisfy the on-site experience. Most of the projects were not permanent installations at ARTPARK; the photographs would become the only future these works would have.

Richard Kelly's *Structure Image/After Image* was shown in two photographs and a small model for the work. The work consisted of a steel cylinder frame 10 feet in diameter and eight feet high. This frame had eight slot openings— four of them were cut up from the bottom of the cylinder, and four cut down from the top. The slot openings were seven inches wide and they prohibited entry. A viewer at ARTPARK could look through the slots at an interior arrangement of concrete blocks. This describes the "structure image" of the title which Kelly calls the work's "first state."[1] The second state, "after image," appeared when the materials were removed from the site— the grass showed an imprint of the structure, or what Kelly called "a surface-stained grid" caused by "the inability of concrete and steel to generate photosynthesis."[2]

Kelly's work was architectural, but a viewer was unable to enter the inner space. The work acted on the site. While the work was materially present, it was sculptural; when it was removed, it left a mark, a sign of its former presence.

Summer Portage by Jeffrey Brosk was clearly architectural in form, as was Kit-Yin Snyder's project. Brosk's wooden grid-like structure of horizontals, verticals and diagonals was painted selectively— the supporting verticals and horizontals were painted black, diagonals were blue, and the steps and upper platforms were red. There was a red, blue and black embellishment and the concrete block buttresses (white in the photographs) were trimmed with red brick. The work's two stairways referred to the "portage" of the title, and the visitor who climbed the structure did so to experience it and to view the natural surroundings. This work recalled the architecture of De Stijl and the international style. Kit-Yin Snyder's *Siciliana* was a work of columns and arches constructed with wire-mesh bricks. Snyder, born in Canton, China, had chosen to work within the Western tradition of architecture. The transparent bricks made the work linear, even calligraphic; the work suggested ruins or traditional Western architecture exposed.

Photographs of Jay Coogan's project showed a group of separate pieces dispersed over a large area. The pieces, made of styrofoam with a concrete surface, were like a stand of trees. The pieces stood vertically or they were arched shapes that sprang upward, then returned to the ground, creating the illusion that they were connected underground. They appeared to penetrate the earth in one place and to emerge again in another.

Scott Burton's work, *Concrete Picnic Table and Benches*, was represented by extensive photo-documentation showing the stages of its development and the completed installation. It was one of the few works that was installed permanently at ARTPARK. It consisted of one large and four small pyramid-shaped concrete forms. Each was inverted and partly buried in the ground, making the flat top of the "table" with "benches" on each of its sides. This work was monumental, and it was furniture. But Burton had placed the four benches very close to the table making it impossible for a person to sit facing another across the table; rather, a person would sit facing nature, viewing the surroundings.

The straight lines and flat planes of Burton's piece made it a minimalist sculpture, but by inverting the pyramids the work appeared to be functional. The work became a tool for social interaction and communion with nature.

Robert Booth's project was called *Dancing Chairs*. Booth filled a field with painted wooden chairs. Each chair was attached by one of its legs to a steel rod, then the rod was planted in the ground. Each chair was set at a slight angle and was elevated well above the level of the ground. This created the sense that the chairs were dancing. Colour was used to compete with nature without isolating the work from it. Each of the planes of the chairs was painted a different colour: red, yellow, blue, orange, green and purple. The choice of the primary and secondary colours, that is, complete colour, turned this group of incongruous dancing chairs toward nature.

Booth contributed three sculptures to the ARC exhibition that relate to his ARTPARK project. One of these, *Shadow Patch,* was a wall-work of miniature chairs on steel wire rods which were imbedded in the wall. The "shadows" were, in fact, flat wooden cut-outs attached to the wall and their contours were the shapes of the shadows of the suspended miniature chairs. The chairs and their shadows were painted blue with orange dots. Booth's choice of colour again was complete, that is, a complementary pair.

Vito Acconci's *SUB-URB* was the most fully documented work exhibited. Photographs, drawings and hand-lettered captions (32 pieces in all) were displayed. Acconci further articulated the work— its inception, its manufacture and its social ramifications— when he visited Toronto to do a workshop and slide lecture during the exhibition.

SUB-URB was a critical social statement. The piece appeared to be a long house with a pitched roof that had been inverted and inserted in the ground so that the roof became a stepped floor. The work, then, was a pit about 100 feet long and 20 feet wide. The house was divided into seven small rooms and seven stairways on each side of a central corridor. The walls of the corridor were painted with stars on one side and stripes on the other. Beside each room was its stepped entrance and a gate; when opened, the gate blocked the corridor. When people entered the rooms of the house, they altered the space, partitioning it. The more people visiting the house, the more the space was divided until each person was isolated. When a viewer explored a small room, he discovered another smaller room beside it in the alcove under the steps of the entrance. The floors of all the rooms were stepped (it was an upside-down house). On the walls of the first small room was a large silhouette of an animal. The second smaller room contained two benches, both of which had been made to be uncomfortable for a viewer who sat down to read the gridded walls that were covered with letters of words. Acconci was using sign and symbol, the American flag, targets, animals, messages in letters scattered on grids, astroturf ("less real, but more perfect"), "to challenge the concept of the suburb as a community."[3]

In his lecture at ARC, Acconci clarified the meanings he intended to convey in *SUB-URB*[4]; he discussed his critical stance as it was reflected in the work. Questions from the audience, especially from those who had visited ARTPARK and experienced the work on site, revealed responses to it that were outside Acconci's intentions. For example: the inverted house was not always recognized; rather, it was perceived to be a boat or an ark (the animal motif supported this), a bunker or an archaeological dig. On site, *SUB-URB* was playful, a game of exploration, and it was a puzzle. The lecture was essential to the work. This exposes a problem common to critical art; that is, ambiguities mislead and the conceptual or cultural boundaries of some symbols are confusing. Acconci's "*long* house," for example, symbolized the suburb, a place where people could not group as they would in the city; it meant segregation and isolation. For native peoples of North America, *longhouse* means community. Acconci's symbol was circumscribed by his own cultural boundary.

Acconci's earlier work sprang from his person and personality. The body-works of the early 1970s and the later performance pieces contrast to the constructed works of the 1980s. In an article based on an interview with Acconci, Ellen Schwartz writes: "He no longer does live pieces because [he says], 'it seemed to me that as long as I was there... the work couldn't get beyond my personality.' His later work is more sociological than psychological."[5] Acconci's recent work seems to this writer to be both sociological and psychological. His works function like performance whether he is present to perform or the viewers act out his performance. Acconci's use of symbol as analogue in *SUB-URB* puts him on shaky ground.

Miho Sawada's *Parelion* at ARTPARK was represented by five drawings and seven photographs. The work consisted of three curved walls, each eight feet high and about 130 feet long. The walls were parallel to each other and their curve described 180 degrees of an ellipse. The walls formed two curved passages or open corridors. The outer and inner walls stood upright; they were made of a wooden frame covered with translucent fiberglass. The centre wall was sloped and it was covered with mylar sheeting. Sawada put a slight twist in the mylar sheet so it would conform to the angle of the sun at different times of the day. The sunlight was reflected from the mylar wall onto the fiberglass walls. Viewers who walked along the passages experienced sunlight and shadow and saw their own reflections on the mylar. Sawada's intention was to create an environment in which to contemplate oneself and the universe.

Sawada added a new installation to the exhibition at ARC. *Dressing Room* was made with a wooden frame eight feet high, three feet wide and 12 feet long. Sheets of corrugated fiberglass were attached to both long sides of the framework; the ends were open, creating a passageway. There were three doors in the passageway dividing it into four spaces, two of which were enclosed cubicles. The doors' wooden frames were covered with mylar. The gallery lights were set so that a viewer entering the passage would cause light to be reflected through the fiberglass from the mylar when he opened each door. The viewer entered, was confined in the first cubicle, confined again in the second cubicle, then set free when he passed through the third door. Of this work, Sawada wrote: "... doors [separate] private and public, inside and outside... In *Dressing Room*, even after closing [the door], one cannot feel free; rather, one is confronted with two opposing values... self and the world outside, reality and illusion, stillness and motion."[6]

The exhibition at ARC was difficult, but rewarding for the patient viewer. Sawada chose to show artists whose works were statements about the social environment, about place and self. In the curator's introduction to the exhibition, Sawada included this quote by Jean-Paul Sartre on freedom and responsibility:

> Thus there are no accidents in a life; a community event which suddenly bursts forth and involves me in it does not come from outside. If I am mobilized in a war, this war is my war; it is my image and I deserve it...[7]

1984

Notes:

1. Statement by the Artist. June, 1981.

2. Ibid.

3. Acconci Lecture at ARC, Toronto, March 10, 1984.

4. Acconci's title is taken from the word "suburb," meaning an outlying district of a city. Acconci associated the suburb with evil. He said that in a city people could group, discuss, argue and even cause revolution; therefore, "they had to put people out in the suburb." (There was no antecedent to *they* in the lecture.) Acconci said that the "sub" portion of the title meant "underground." He did not deal with the "urb" portion of the title. The hyphenated parts meant "suburb."

5. "Vito Acconci: 'I Want To Put The Viewer On Shaky Ground.'" by Ellen Schwartz. *ARTnews*, Summer, 1981.

6. Statement by the Artist. March, 1984.

7. Jean-Paul Sartre. *Existentialism and Human Emotions*. New York, Philosophical Library (Wisdom Library), 1957.

How I See Andreas Gehr.

The New City of Sculpture was held in six Toronto centres in August and September of this year. More than 50 works by 33 local artists were chosen for exhibit by curators David Clarkson and Robert Wiens. The exhibition was mounted to focus on Toronto as a major centre of sculptural practice.

The exhibition was an event. It made public the event of sculptural activity in Toronto. Each work exhibited was an *event* created by an individual artist. This article will focus on the work exhibited by Andreas Gehr.

Gehr's *Untitled 1984* was shown at ARC. The installation occupied the signature wall of the larger gallery. The work was made up of four parts—three separate sculptural pieces and a printed sheet. The central sculptural part of this work was a ziggurat-like construction that abutted and advanced from the wall on which it was mounted. The "steps" of this piece were made of an opaque black reflective material alternating with a matte black heat-warped metal. White paint had been applied to the matte surfaces in a dense pattern that suggested ancient hieroglyphic markings. On the reflective black surfaces (which were vertical) were configurations of inlaid mother-of-pearl in two places. The vertical surfaces contrasted with the matte metal surfaces (the obliques of the construction), but they, too, had been made reflective by the white patterns painted on them.

To the right of this ziggurat-like piece hung a hand-brushed aluminum shape on which white configurations and a red marking had been made. This piece was flat. Its right side was rectangular; that is, it had a vertical edge and horizontal edges at top and bottom. On the left side, closest to the ziggurat-like construction, the edge of the shape was "stepped." Vertical and diagonal edges alternated obliquely from top to bottom making the aluminum plane wider at its top than at its bottom. The contour on the left side of this piece repeated the contour of the central construction.

The markings applied to the aluminum piece were figurative. Small opaque white human figures and tree or flower-like shapes were strategically placed on the surface to suggest a random pattern. At the centre of the plane was a red line; its topmost part was a short horizontal, then it turned 90 degrees, becoming a short vertical, then proceeded downward in a regular and most beautiful double curve ending sharply as another horizontal. This line would have appeared to be incised, but the artist had brushed white paint under and around it to maintain the planar effect on the flat surface of the aluminum. The red line suggested the outline of one side of a vase.

To the left of the central construction, a small vertical rectangle was mounted. On it, a photographed image had been printed. The image was a figure on a cross. The figure appeared to have been made of metal; the metal face was featureless and the head, hands and feet had been pressed flat. The figure had been bound to a wooden cross by an inverted triangle of cloth. It was this object that had been photographed, then printed. The print was the third sculptural piece in the installation.

These three sculptural pieces can be interpreted in terms of the historical clues given in them. The central ziggurat could relate to antiquity— Mesopotamia, Babylon or Egypt. But the white pattern is only suggestive, not specific, and the inlaid configurations seem both ancient and modern. The aluminum piece with its figures and the outline of a vase could refer to the Greek era, and the printed photograph, to the crucified Christ. One could extrapolate on the symbolic emblems on these constructions, but I will not do so here. I believe that the meaning of Andreas Gehr's work is not to be found by tracing references, or interpreting its signs and symbols. The work is not a matter of semiotics; it is a sculpture, a piece of visual art. This is how I see it.

In describing the three pieces, I have tried to state directly what each one was. It is the object as action, as artifact, as *event* that I have tried to write down. I believe that description, by itself, is critical— the words that a writer chooses to describe a work of art reveal his concepts about that work. To pursue symbolic referents is to digress from the work. A review of the historical meaning of symbols is a dissertation on a subject *other than* the artwork at hand.

I think it is significant that Gehr's constructions did not imitate an actual ziggurat, a Greek vase or the crucifixion. I think it is important to look at what he did. The ziggurat-like construction is black and white. It reflects and absorbs light in two ways: black absorbs and white reflects light, and the matte surface absorbs and the smooth surface reflects light. The construction is not free-standing— it is a mounted wall relief. The central piece states its own fundamental principles. The actual sculptural properties of this part of the installation are unlike any historical equivalent. Differences outnumber samenesses. The aluminum piece with white figures and the red line that describes the outline of a vase is uncompromisingly planar, unlike a three-dimensional vase. Here, difference is eminent. The photographed image of the flattened figure and cross, even the visible pentagonal shape of the cloth that binds the two parts, is a print of the photographed construction.

If these pieces are not to be viewed as symbols of antiquity, the Greek and Christian eras, why do they have this appearance? How do I see it? I think Gehr's installation states that the ziggurat, the vase and the cruciform are each sculptural forms, and it is this relationship that is relevant. The act of creating, visible in Gehr's pieces, is generated by the same creative impulse that has moved artists in all eras, and the materials and methods of making and marking have historical parallels. The reference that is important is a non-symbolic one; it is the basic sculptural principle in Gehr's work and in the works of history. I believe that Andreas Gehr is not pointing backward to history, but forward. This installation has been made to state its own meaning and this artist's personal mythology.

Gehr's personal mythology is his legacy as an artist. Gehr may, or may not, be a student of historical art; he may, or may not, have a thorough knowledge of the art of the ancient world, the Greek and the Christian eras. He *is* an artist. What he claims as an artist is the inheritance of all art that precedes him. He is informed by its presence; like all other artists, he is the legatee of the art of the past. Gehr's sculptures reveal his claim, his legacy, his individual mythology and *proclaim* it; they reveal his sensibility and his understanding of all that he has known. I don't believe that Gehr is making art to direct viewers toward some other art; rather, he is making art *unlike* any other art. The installation at ARC has not been made before. This is how I see it.

Sculpture, like painting, is pre-linguistic. It addresses the senses, the eye and mind of the viewer. It is a manifestation of the sensibility, the eye and mind of the artist. To interpret Gehr's installation as a semiotic entity, encoded with sign and symbol, ignores the essential, fundamental meaning of the work. However, Gehr knows that signs are useful, and one was posted as the fourth part of this work. It is reproduced here in its entirety:

Some Possible Titles

What an immense contradiction between
the conventional experience of art
and the autonomous sculpture!

Interpretation misunderstands the
relativity of sculpture.

We use signs as if they were the
real things for which they stand.

Obstinacy in the face of logical
judgement.

In sculpture one lives to create
confusion, without direction, without
responsibility— and this is good.
To let oneself be surprised requires
innocence.

Sculpture shows that usefulness is not
very useful if you succeed in becoming
a child.

We lose sight of the action by watching
only for the signs of meaning.
Action is the syntax of the sculpture.

Crass sculptures are recognizable
by their good reasons.

With regard to what are we to compare
sculptures? Neither the sculpture nor
interpretation have any fixed point.
Each is beyond itself and the other.

Thought and feeling are limit notions
of the same thing. Despite dualism.

Sculptures die when they try to exceed
their own poetics.

Each sculpture has its own grammar-in-
action.

This sheet of possible titles encouraged me to write about this work. I hoped to show by my writing something fundamental to the work, and fundamental to this artist. This article is not an interpretation or a critical analysis; rather, I have written what I believe is the *event* of the work.

It has become customary for art writers to disregard the event of a work in favour of their own responses and ideas. Their method has influenced some artists to make art that satisfies the conventions of symbolic interpretation. Visual art is essentially perceptual. An artist's tools are his eyes, his intuition, his intellect and the materials he uses. Artists can, and do, use words, slogans, signs and written messages to impress on viewers the presence and meaning of their works. The viewer can read, but he must look; he must notice everything. Everything is important.

I don't know Andreas Gehr. I have never met him, nor have I ever spoken with him. I don't believe I need to meet this artist to see his work. The installation at ARC was complete. I had the opportunity to view it again and again over the period of the exhibition. This is how I saw it.

1984

Who Are You, Greg Curnoe?

Greg Curnoe's exhibition, *Rubber Stamp Books and Works 1961-1989*, at Art Metropole, gave a rare opportunity to viewers. One cannot speak of Curnoe's *oeuvre* without including this rubber-stamp work. Over 30 items were displayed in glass cases, and 30 more works were framed and hung on the walls.

The seven *Blue Books*, made from 1964 to 1972, were shown opened. These are tall blue ledgers in which Curnoe has printed lists of words, making each book a unique hand-stamped narrative. In these books and on other pages, the texts accumulate to give a portrayal of the artist's concerns, his curiosities and his knowledge.

Concurrent with the exhibition was the release of Curnoe's *Blue Book 8*. This document, hand-stamped between December 7, 1988, and October 2, 1989, was published by Art Metropole; it is the only blue book to be made available in an edition. The book is a faithful facsimile of Curnoe's rubber-stamped pages. The last words on the last page of the text speak for all of Curnoe's rubber-stamped works— "to be continued."

Curnoe often works on found pieces of paper. This gives his works an archival appearance. His lists are deceptively simple and his titles are direct: *Favourite American Singers*, or *French Artists* and *List of Names of Boys I Grew Up With*. Some texts seem humourous, but they question what they address— like the three works titled *Slogan*, and those called *Contradiction*.

This show was selected by the artist. It presents his own history, his relationship to other histories, and it shows his interaction with everything that passes his door. Curnoe has been formed and informed by his life, his loves and his labours; he has transformed these things and made his art. A list of names is a poem; hand-stamped on a page, it is a work of art. These works show Curnoe's awareness of the ultimate importance of the particular.

It would be a mistake to regard any of the works in this exhibition as ephemeral— they are not. The rubber-stamped letter, word, list of words, sentence or text has been at the heart of Curnoe's work from its beginnings. These are small works, but they are no less important for their size. In fact, the size and the materials and the means employed make them an intimate encounter with Curnoe's thought for any viewer who is open to his work. Clearly, art and life are understood to be one for this artist and that struggle that is called "existential" can be seen here.

One has to wonder why Curnoe's work has not been shown regularly in Toronto over the past decade. A proud Canadian artist, he is concerned with the health of this country. Curnoe is a painter; his work shows that his concerns are populist, nationalist, social, political and cultural. His work is figurative; it is textual, and it is accessible. As a critical artist, he is thoughtful and literate. He seems, to this viewer, to have been a singularly well qualified leader for young artists throughout the 1980s. It is a pity that he has not been seen to play that role for Canada to which he is particularly adept. In the 1980s, when Germany astutely recognized Joseph Beuys in its midst, Canada looked abroad for leaders and left fallow the work of Greg Curnoe.

1990

Guido Molinari: The Formative Years.

The exhibition of Guido Molinari's early paintings at the Art Gallery of Ontario this summer gave Toronto viewers a chance to learn of the formative work in this artist's development. The show is a landmark exhibit by an artist whose work is often said to be esoteric in the extreme. In these works, Molinari shows us the core of his visual thinking and the sources of his mature perception.

The earliest work, *Untitled 1951,* and the final work in the chronology of the selection, *Hommage à Jouran 1961*, are what we call "colour works." The first led to the enquiry addressed by the body of work shown; the last announces the resolution of vertical form and pure colour familiar to viewers of Molinari's paintings since the 1960s. These two works hang like parentheses around the body of thought evident in this show. We see, in the young Molinari, the emerging consciousness of colour, its energy and its behaviour; we see the experiential examination of pictorial event in those works that give the show its title, *The Black and White Paintings*.

For a painter, black and white are colours. These pigments have particular qualities; they have a particular relationship that occurs in no other colour pair. Together, they present an extreme contrast by which the plane (or planes) may be determined. Using black and white, a painter creates one, two, or one and one and one (and so on), articulating the surface event of a painting. In this exhibition, Molinari's black and white works show a stringently uncompromising examination of the energy of form and colour, and because they are black and white, they are the most directly unified works in the show.

Much has been written about the paintings that Molinari made while blindfolded to explore automatism. This show includes one such work. The colour works that followed this experiment are numerous in this selection and are of greater importance. They show the young Molinari searching form with colour. It is noticeable that he favoured red, yellow, orange and green (blue, although present, does not report as a whole colour in these works). In the earliest works, the colour is applied in strokes, that is, drawing with paint is evident; then, the paint is laid on the surface as "blobs," that is, amorphous shapes, each of one solid colour made rich with loaded brush strokes, make up the painting. There follow paintings with greater order in which colour is better described as shapes that abut each other and divide the surface into areas of colour that interact with each other. In all of these works, the organization is irregular; they search for equilibrium with anxious, awkward means. *Angle Rouge 1955* appears to be a breakthrough; it is a synthesis of colour and order, shape and direction on the painted plane, and it is shown here as the harbinger of the black and white paintings.

When Molinari reduced colour to black and white, he gave himself the opportunity to both explore and exploit his vision at its most fundamental level. *Trinoir 1955* and *Quadrinoir 1955* predate *Binoir* and we see in this process of reduction a consciousness of *one and one and one*. *Binoir* and *Triblanc* were made in 1955. In 1956, *Uninoir* (both the work on paper and the painting by this title) and *Blanc Encerclant* began a new examination of irregular shapes and the equivalence of the plane. A series of works on paper, realized again as paintings on canvas, were made in 1956. These seem to culminate in *Quadriblanc 1956* and *Angle Noir 1956*.

The titles for these works were thoughtfully chosen; they express an aspect of the visual event of each painting. Neither the titles nor the paintings are about calculation or counting, but they could be said to be about *number* as that concept occurs in modernist and ancient thought. These simple black and white works demand viewing over and over again. Seeing is thinking; it is a non-verbal form of thought. These works embody the thought and the vision which is Molinari's painting vocabulary.

Huit Blanc 1958 seems to gather into itself the properties of the earlier black and white works. In it, there is a tendency toward the horizontal and the vertical, but the black shape is, in fact, always oblique. The eight white shapes are irregular, and no white shape is the same as any other. The painting functions as an equivalent and, at the same time, the whole work unifies.

Opposition no. 2 1959 is a colour work and its two black areas are in horizontal/vertical opposition to each other. *Vertical Horizontal Blancs 1960*, with red, yellow and blue, shows that Molinari has turned from searching form with colour to searching colour with form. The final work reduces form to verticality; in this work, colour (red and blue and black and white) is the active force which articulates the whole painting.

The greater part of this exhibition was chosen from 1955-56. These two years of Molinari's formative period seem to have been the densest in work and in thought. The colour works and the black and white paintings made in those years represent a virtual explosion of vision, and they show a careful search into the elements of painting. The catalogue that accompanies the exhibition includes a short essay by Molinari entitled "The 'Blob' Space or The Automatism Situation" originally published in 1955 in the Montreal newspaper *L'Autorité du peuple*. It was translated by Molinari in 1988 and it appears in the exhibition catalogue for the first time in English. Read it; Molinari is the best writer on his own thought and work.

1990

The Robert Downing Archive.

> I admonish all who have any knowledge of these matters that they write it down. Do it truly and plainly, not toilsomely and at great length, for the sake of those who seek and are glad to learn.
>
> Albrecht Dürer

In 1986, *The Robert Downing Archive* was acquired by the Art Gallery of Hamilton. The archive was donated to the Gallery by a Toronto businessman by arrangement and in agreement with the artist. Thus, the Gallery at Hamilton (Downing's hometown) received over 140 works that represent 20 years of this senior Canadian artist's production.

The archive is a vast collection of artwork and documentary material. Downing is a sculptor, a designer, a researcher, a teacher, a photographer and a writer, and in all these areas his approach is aggressive and highly innovative. An inventory of the entire archive shows that it includes 22 sculptures and eight relief works, 88 two-dimensional works and 23 documentary works. These last mainly take the form of books (large three-ring binders) packed full of typed or hand-printed pages with photographs or illustrations. Downing calls them "DOCUmeditation WORKS," and a single work may consist of up to six volumes.

Last year, the Downing archive was opened to Montreal writer Jennifer Fisher who examined it for the purpose of an exhibition. Fisher, as guest curator for the last of a series of exhibitions initiated by Ihor Holubizky, curator at the Hamilton Gallery, chose 35 items for exhibit that were representative of the archive and of her response to it. From 19 November 1991 to 12 January 1992, the exhibition was open for viewing at the Art Gallery of Hamilton under the title *Curatorial Laboratory Project #8: DUCU-meditations. The Robert Downing Archive*, and I was able to see it.

Robert Downing became prominent on the Toronto art scene in 1967.

That year of Centennial celebrations gave unprecedented opportunities to many Canadian artists and Downing was among them. In partnership with Ted Bieler, he created the concrete curtain wall designs for the exterior of the Medical Science Building at the University of Toronto, and he added to that building two concrete sculpted walls and a mandala of his own. From 1966 to 1968, Downing was making cube-related sculptures that were shown at the Dunkelman Gallery in Toronto and the Agnes Lefort Gallery in Montreal. This "Cube Series" (108 works) brought about the invitation to exhibit at the Whitechapel Art Gallery in London, England, in 1969, making Downing the first Canadian artist to have a solo exhibition at a major European gallery. In 1971, his works were among those selected to represent Canada at the 11th Biennale of Middleheim in Antwerp, Belgium. In 1972, an exhibition of Downing's sculpture toured six Ontario galleries. (I saw this show at the Rothman Gallery in Stratford.) Downing moved to California (1974-1978) to work and teach, but his work could still be seen in Toronto. He received commissions in Canada and in the United States until the 1980s when we, the viewing public, lost sight of him.

Where has Robert Downing been throughout the 1980s? Between periods spent in Toronto, Montreal and back in Toronto again, he has been in Botswana and Singapore teaching and lecturing on sculpture and three-dimensional design. What has he been doing? While it is well-known that Downing is a sculptor, it is not known (and if known, not well understood) that he is a *conceptual* artist. Throughout the 1980s Downing has been involved in a series of conceptual-visual-language projects that are so directly critical, so consciously committed to action and purpose that they make other forms of art about critical issues pale by comparison. Downing developed his critical art from the circumstances of his life, the particulars of his time and this country. He examined the cultural and educational climate in Canada, and he made of his thoughts and actions what he has come to call "socially integrated conceptual/performance works." He did this by writing, by teaching, by compiling; he did it by graphic means; he did it by advertisement, and he did it by addressing directly our governments, corporations and cultural institutions.

By definition, a "socially integrated conceptual/performance work" addresses society so that society will act or react (participate) in it. Such a work may involve conventional or radical means to stimulate response, but *no predetermined response is expected*. The work is set at large (released) or specifically directed, but its consequence, its ramifications and repercussions occur at the will of the recipient. Since 1979, Downing has developed six such projects. Among the "DOCUmeditation WORKS" in the archive at Hamilton, full documentation of three of them can be found. A careful examination of the entire archive will show that *The Robert Downing Archive*, itself, is also one of them.

In light of this, it is fitting that the exhibition at Hamilton carry Ihor Holubizky's banner *Curatorial Laboratory Project #8*. It is appropriate that Jennifer Fisher should select the show and introduce it as an experience of discovery, and for my part, it follows that having seen the exhibition, I should write about it here.

For the exhibition, Jennifer Fisher chose 10 of the 22 sculptures in the archive and 10 of the 88 two-dimensional works. From the 23 "DOCUmeditation WORKS," she showed 15 of the books mounted on sloping shelves for reading access, and two multi-part works called *Artist's Sample Case and Seal* and *I.B.M. Model* which she displayed in a large glass-topped display case. Fisher's selection favoured Downing's written material (the books), and although it was difficult, it was not impossible to grasp the content/context of the show. I saw (and read) the exhibition over three visits.

Fisher was particularly interested by the document titled *Feeling My Way*. This text is a version of Downing's autobiography. Fisher chose excerpts from it, reproduced them in large type as one continuous text of 40 pages and mounted these pages along three walls of the gallery. Below Downing's text and parallel to it, she mounted her own 39-page text which described her discovery of the archive, her interest in it and her response to it. In her text, Fisher characterized Downing as "a male artist who came of age in the sixties generation," and described herself: "I am a woman critic writing in the nineties." She posits "a gap... that will always be there due to our separate histories" between Downing and herself which "opens a metaphoric space within which the exhibition is constituted." I wish to dispute this "gap" and "metaphoric space." As a viewer/reader of the exhibition and a willing participant in a "socially integrated conceptual/performance work," I have a few thoughts to the contrary.

The differences of age, gender and personal history that separate Robert Downing and Jennifer Fisher were powerless to prevent Fisher from participating in this work. The human sentiment of Downing's writing touched her deeply. While she speaks of a gap, she actually closes it with her own writing. She responded to Downing's art with her own, to his humanity with hers. Fisher, if not a writer of the 1980s, must surely have been a student of the 1980s. Downing, today at 56 years of age, is also an artist and student of the 1980s. The archive includes a large number of works that were conceived and made during the 1980s; it covers *only* 20 years of Downing's activity. I see no meaningful gap, and so, no metaphoric space. What Fisher has done with this exhibition is real and concrete— she has taken the first step in opening Downing's art with all its complexity, its detail and its interconnectedness for an audience who will not have seen the likes of it before.

On entering the exhibition rooms, I first gave my attention to Downing's sculpture. The first large works in view were *Alpha & Omega* (1967), a cube-related work (the maquette, reproduced in aluminum) and *N.P.1(b)* (1975/7), a spiral column (one of the eight sculptures that make up the "Nothing Series" or "Fibonacci Series"). In a smaller gallery off the main exhibition space, I found *Nothing Plus W2* (1975/6) and *N.P.3* (1975/7) along with *N.P.2* (1975/7) and a small work titled *G.* (1975/7). On the floor lay *W2 or Something* (1975/81), a large red "ring." These works were made of fiberglass-reinforced-polyester and variously finished. The curious forms and the coded titles of these works would take on their true meaning when I perused the rest of the exhibition.

On display in the main gallery, beside an unfinished casting of a maquette for a work that Downing abandoned, I found the small solid bronze "maquette" *Nothing* (1974/5), the first work in the "Nothing Series." This tiny "ring" (about 6" diam.) stands upright on its edge. Downing calls it a "geometric bronze crystal." It is the key, the seminal work, for the entire "Fibonacci Series" and a revelation in itself. (But I would learn about this later when I read the documents.)

Because I am familiar with Downing's "Cube Series," I was drawn to the five bromide prints related to that work. *Drawing #1* (1966/7) and four *Studies on a Cube* (1967) were grouped together. Elsewhere, *L Panel* (1967), an ink drawing, the original design for the fifth floor panels on the exterior of the U. of T. Medical Sciences Building, was displayed beside *Birthday Suite VI* (1975), a work I would understand better when I learned of the "I'Ching Series."

Next, I turned to a shelf of six books. These six volumes comprise a teaching vehicle or "textbook" which Downing developed as an "exploration of elemental morphology." The contents are an encyclopaedic visual discourse on form using coloured graphics, photographs and text. This work, called *Transentials of Space* or *Ti*, was created to teach or train students in three-dimensional competence using two-dimensional means. It is designed for multi-media access; it can be reproduced on film or video for computer display, or it can be reproduced in book-form by any standard black and white or colour copy machine. The copy at the Art Gallery of Hamilton is one of five produced on a Canon 400 Colour Copier. Downing worked on *Ti* every day for two years (1981-1983). The original set of six volumes which is elegantly housed in a lacquered black box designed to offer up one volume at a time, remains in the artist's possession. Downing considers *Ti* to be "the most significant artwork of my life, so far."

At the centre of the gallery, was a reading station which held nine large volumes. I understood that they, along with *Ti*, were "DOCUmeditation WORKS." I opened a binder to find all of the catalogues for all of the exhibitions of Downing's work. Another binder held his reviews; I read through this quickly and was impressed by the scope of the interest taken in Downing's work from 1966 to 1978. Kay Kritzwiser's reviews for the Toronto *Globe and Mail* (1968-71) and Anita Aarons' article in *Artscanada* (1968) might be expected, but Ken Woods writing for *Fiberglass Report* and H. Thomasson for *Fabricators Journal* (1968) were news for me. There were articles from Los Angeles (1975) and one in *Canadian Architect* (1978). For the catalogue of the show at Whitechapel Gallery in England, Dennis Young wrote an introductory essay. The show received three newspaper reviews, among them, Paul Overy's in the *London Financial Times*. Bryan Robertson wrote about the show for *Studio International* (August 1969), and Edward Lucie-Smith and Patricia White for *Art In Britain*. I knew that this compilation was public knowledge, available at a library if one searched for it piece by piece. I opened another binder. It was dated *June 4/70*, titled *A Lecture for International Summer School. Fanshawe College, London, Ontario. By Robert James Downing*. Another page showed another title, *An Outline of Events and a Summary of Facts Relative to my July-August 1969 Exhibition at the Whitechapel Art Gallery*. I had hit pay-dirt.

The Fanshawe lecture is a 26-page typescript that traces the development of the "Cube Series." Downing describes his thinking for these works and gives technical details. The works were not made without a struggle. The narrative is an account of Downing's work and his career from 1966 to 1970. It gives a portrait of the artistic environment in Toronto in those years, a time of high expectations, promising activity, but merciless public indifference. As I read, I was impressed by Downing's professionalism. He made the "Cube Series" out of artistic necessity and he risked everything for it. He established a workshop-studio bringing a plastics craftsman and an aluminum welder to work on the premises, and he made their skills available to other sculptors. He opened a showroom, had exhibitions with established galleries, but his sales were not enough to relieve the huge debt that was accumulating. For the Whitechapel show, Downing sold his house to pay transportation costs for the 74 works he took to England. He showed there to great acclaim. He returned home to work and teach to earn the money "to bring my sculpture back to Canada." For those who believe that the 1960s was a golden era for Canadian artists, there is a truer story here. For those of the 1980s generation who call that decade a myth, these pages are a succinct and lucid record of the 1960s as *lived experience*. It is a sobering text.

Of the two collage works in the show, one combines the period of the 1960s with the experience of the 1980s. *Time* (1984) shows a copy of the article on Downing published in the Canadian issue of *Time Magazine*

(February 9, 1968) beside a cover from the magazine (March 5, 1984) on which Downing has made a painting of one of his own sculptures. Of this work, he says: "... in recent years... an artist must 'compete' and become a 'salesperson' if they wish to 'succeed.' This work suggests the untruth of [that] prevailing social belief. The cover is, of course, a forgery, but that is considered to be OK... as opposed to... an illegal breach of copyright laws, and the article, which is real, is poorly written and full of the writer's warped view of my 'reality'... contributing nothing toward my present success as an artist." One can call this cynical or philosophical, or both, but it is based on firm grounds.

I browsed the document *Some Letters* (1979/80) and got a sketch of a major *societal* project which is the basis for Downing's "socially integrated conceptual/performance works." Downing is a quintessential teacher because he is an eternal student of life and the world. With the help of a team of management consultants, he wrote letters to the presidents of 500 Canadian corporations. Positive results came in contracts with I.B.M. Canada Ltd. "to research and develop a travelling exhibition depicting elementary geometrical structural principles..." and with Texaco Canada Inc. "to prepare a cultural policy, and then assist in the formulation of their Art Collection Program." *Some Letters* is a 251-page compilation of the material accumulated during these dubious teaching/learning experiences. It connects with the multi-part work, *I.B.M. Model* (1979); it led Downing to write the autobiography, *Finding My Way*, and ultimately, to create the six volume *Transentials of Space* (1981/83).

Corporate Canada's message was received and understood by Downing and in 1984, as part of what he calls the "Closet Art Series," he gathered *Artist's Sample Case and Seal* (1966/84). This briefcase was displayed opened. Downing describes it: "It contains examples of all the materials that an artist is expected to give away in today's society if they hope to remain in 'business.' Contents of this 'travelling exhibition' include: business cards, slides, pamphlets, copies of reviews, and among several more things, even a 'piece' of the artist." Downing regards this assemblage as a sculpture. Of the sculptures represented in it, he explains: "It was while I was assembling this work... that I recognized how sculpture that had been lost or destroyed over the years, combined with misplaced or damaged negatives, had inadvertently turned single photos into unique artworks. In some cases, the documentation records an artwork that existed in the past simply for the purpose of manifesting one photoprint now."

Downing's work after 1970 is less well-known than are his earlier cube-related sculptures. In 1970, he began to explore the graphic potential of the cube as a two-dimensional form. I am familiar with Downing's mandalas (not in this exhibition); they are meticulously crafted contemplative works. In the exhibition, I found what I regard to be the source of Downing's iconography. There were two binders, each a hand-written document/journal, which give complete accounts of Downing's work and his thinking from 1970 to 1978. (Downing moved to Long Beach, California, in 1974 where he worked and taught at the California State University at Long Beach; he returned to Canada at the end of 1978) In my opinion, these two books are the most important documents in the archive.

The book titled *The I'Ching Series* is a notebook that Downing began writing in August of 1975. It records the details of a direction he pursued from 1970 to 1976. He wanted to find a two-dimensional image that would undergo *change* as one looked at it. From his study of the cube module, he knew that an isometric projection of the cube gave a hexagon. He was familiar with the ancient *Book of Changes* or *I'Ching* and its hexagrams. When he chose to work with the hexagon, he was working essentially with the cube; he was combining an aspect of a three-dimensional solid with its two-dimensional shape.

The work took two courses— one pursued his concerns for interrelationship and order; the other, generated by the vast number of design elements he brought to bear on the repeated hexagonal unit, was to develop an educational game for all ages and to have it mass produced. The game's hexagonal unit Downing called a "cosmicomic continuant." It was supplied as coloured stickers, rubber stamps and as stencils, allowing a user to create an endless variety of patterned artworks on his own. The project held great promise. Downing produced the trial *Cosmokit* in 18 copies (not in this exhibition), began proceedings for a patent, but in the end, the project was abandoned. His research, however, was invaluable and he continued to work with his own hexagonal designs, constructing a series of two-dimensional works from them. As he progressed, the works and the technical means he used to create them became more complicated and more costly, and in 1976, now deeply involved with his sculpture, he decided to rethink this direction and he shelved it. *Birthday Suite VI* (1975) in this exhibition is a computer produced image as a mounted blueprint, reproduced by Xerox on vellum; it is an incomplete work from the "I'Ching Series."

For Jennifer Fisher, *The Robert Downing Archive* came into focus when she read his autobiography. In her text, she compares her experience to the discovery of an Egyptian tomb. Each day that I visited the exhibition, I looked at the large-scale sculptures. Their configurations puzzled me; they were composed of triangles, squares, trapezoids and pentagons— here was plane geometry in solid construction reconciled with an organic fluidity. On each visit, I would return to the small bronze "ring," *Nothing* (1974/5). It was when I read the second hand-written notebook, *Nothing Series*, that Tutankhamen's tomb opened for me.

Nothing Series, the text, was begun on January 21, 1976. In it, Downing sets down an account of the events that would yield the sculptures that were puzzling me. Downing's work with the cube had been thorough; one early work, *5832* (1967), is "a golden rectangle expression of the cube." Of the sculptures made between 1967 and 1971, Downing separates his concerns into what he calls "The Exploding Cube Series" (18 works), "The Cube Edge Series" (two large works and 24 models), a "Topographical Series" (exploring 2-D and 3-D relationships) and the "Corner Unit Series" (using the cubes' three left and three right forms). In this last series, Downing's corner units were sometimes 1/8 sections of octahedra which, when combined with tetrahedra, make the cube phenomenon. Downing's work with the hexagon, the "I'Ching Series," fully occupied him from 1971 to 1973, then he began a search for forms which would combine the square, the equilateral triangle (six of which form a hexagon) and the pentagon. Downing entered a period of *pure research* combining plane and solid geometries to explore the relationships between three-sided, four-sided, five-sided and six-sided regular plane shapes and their solid crystalloid structures. In March of 1974, he notes his "first breakthrough." (He says "first"— it was *the* breakthrough of a lifetime!)

Downing began with a repeated pentagonal face and built a nine-part ring-shaped solid. When separated, each section of the ring was a crystalloid module showing two pentagons, two equilateral triangles, and *two 108 degree trapezoids*. On examination, he found that the relationship of the trapezoid to the pentagon was in the ratio of the *golden section* (1:1.618). This is also known as the *Fibonacci ratio*, hence, the alternative title "Fibonacci Series." Downing's findings were confirmed by Professor Barron Brainard (Mathematics Department, University of Toronto) who recognized the importance of his discovery and had it recorded in Downing's name. In the notebook, *Nothing Series*, the details of the rigorous thinking and the experiments that led to the discovery are given in spare and simple words. I have not read so exciting an account of discovery since Watson's *Double Helix*.

In the exhibition, *the* module (Downing called it W1) can be seen as the small 6" bronze "ring" sculpture *Nothing*. Downing had continued his search by dissecting the module into as many solids as he could find in it. One section was a prism (called W2) which can be seen in the large red "ring" *W2 or Something*. By combining the module with one or more sections from it and adding a cube, Downing created a series of small models. He made eight large-scale sculptures which he regards as one work. Other works were made as commissions, as models and as out-of-series works. The tendency for these works to spiral is natural (of nature) due to the Fibonacci ratio inherent in the module and it accounts for the organic fluidity that I saw. It is difficult on casual viewing to grasp what is at work in these sculptures; they are informed by unforeseen relationships. However, one recognizes and responds to their fundamental morphology, the "ideal proportion."

It is worth noting that Robert Downing is self-educated; his formal schooling ended at Grade Eight. He has, however, a remarkable intelligence and he has brought a driving passion to his work. His mind is unrestrained by academic conventions, and it may be due to this that he was able to venture with his art unhesitatingly into mathematics and crystallography. In this era of specialization, so free-ranging an intellect is rare. Because

Downing is a sculptor, his method of inquiry was the same as that used by Euclid and Archimedes— he made models with his hands and he noticed how they worked. The ancient Greek mathematicians reasoned and taught with actual prisms, cones and spheres long before the laws of perspective made it possible to draw a volume on a two-dimensional page. But Downing is also a student of the Renaissance which gave us perspective, and he sees in that *gain* of drawing the illusion of a volume on the flat surface, a *loss* of understanding of the actual space of solids. He wanted to teach students to grasp three-dimensional space from the image on the two-dimensional page. With this goal and with the knowledge he had gained from the "Nothing Series," his resolution of plane and solid geometries, he began in 1981 to work on the six volume "textbook" *Transentials of Space*. It is no wonder that he regards this work so highly.

My three days spent looking at *The Robert Downing Archive* were not enough for me to take in the whole exhibition, and that selection was only part of the archive. The archive is no mere collection of papers; the books have been carefully compiled with relevant letters interfiled. The descriptive list of inventory that Downing drew up is a cataloguer's dream— items are detailed and cross-references are given. For students and scholars who will look at the archive, there will be no end of surprises.

For my part in this "socially integrated conceptual/performance work," I thank Ihor Holubizky who showed the archive to Jennifer Fisher for a laboratory project. I thank Jennifer for the exhibition I saw. I am grateful to the adventuresome Toronto businessman whose donation made the exhibition possible, and most of all, I thank Robert Downing who wrote so much down truly and plainly for my sake. To the curators at the Art Gallery of Hamilton in whose custody *The Robert Downing Archive* now resides: I urge you to take good care of it— it's worth millions and millions and millions.

1992

An Essay (1996)

What Colour Are the Gallery Walls?

Reader:

It is my dilemma that I believe I have something to say, but I don't know to whom I should say it. The problem deepens if those who I think should read this, do not; it broadens if those who do read it, don't recognize that this is a serious matter.

I am circulating these thoughts among those few people who might have a reason to be interested, whether or not they agree with what I have written.

If you are one who is disturbed by the question I have raised, take up this issue along with me. If you have not been disturbed by it because you haven't thought about it before, then I urge you, think now. If, after reading this, you believe that what I've said is irrelevant and unimportant, you will be wrong.

For the past six years, I have been seeing coloured walls in art museums. Over this time, the reasoning in support of coloured walls has evolved. Initially, coloured walls were used to evoke the appearance of the rooms in which the art displayed was likely to have hung at the time it was made, or they were intended to create the atmosphere of a period in history. More recently, the idea has been to reassess the art and examine its relevance to current thought. In both cases, the practice is based on theoretical assumptions rather than on observation or experience.

I intend to examine the wisdom (or lack of it) of showing art in rooms with coloured walls. My questions will centre on light and colour, on vision, and ultimately, on knowledge. Art is experiential, and I believe that viewers in public art museums are being denied access to the art they have come to see.

The Art Gallery of Ontario in Toronto figures prominently in this survey for two reasons: it is the art museum that I visit most often, and it is at the forefront of the new display techniques. The AGO curators are not truly leaders however innovative their installations appear. Because their ideas are rooted in theory, they are followers. They ignore the visual consequence of their decorative displays, and by them, degrade the art that it is their responsibility to share.

The first exhibition that I saw on coloured walls was *Lucius R. O'Brien: Visions of Victorian Canada* as it was installed at the AGO in 1990. Each gallery room was painted a different colour. It didn't seem to me then, nor does it now, that the colours belonged to the period of the paintings. The coloured walls were distracting; they impeded my view of the paintings. Fortunately, I was in Ottawa when the O'Brien exhibition was shown at the National Gallery. There, I saw the same paintings on neutral coloured cloth walls. The "jazz" was gone and so was the disturbance caused by the walls at the AGO. At the National Gallery, I saw the actual colours of the paintings. This retrospect of work by the 19th-century Canadian painter was the first ever assembled, and possibly it would be the only chance I would have in my lifetime to see these works gathered together.

My next encounter with coloured walls came in the summer of 1992, again at the AGO. It was a difficult time for the Gallery— cuts to Government funding had caused staff layoffs and the Gallery was about to close until the building of Stage III was completed— but that summer the *AGO News* announced that "the refurbishment and installation of the Old Masters galleries are now complete." The Old Masters galleries, the original gallery rooms of the Art Gallery of Toronto, are at the centre of the present building. They house the European Painting and Sculpture Collection which spans the 15th to the 19th centuries. When I visited the Gallery, I found these rooms painted red-orange, red and yellow. Such high coloration cast coloured light on the artworks. In the yellow room, a painting by Claude Monet was overcast by yellow light reflected from the walls. Was this supposed to imitate sunlight? Monet's delicate work about light and colour was distorted. I was confounded. What were they thinking?

The answer came when Stage III of the building was finished and the AGO reopened in January 1993. The public was invited to "discover the permanent collection in its splendid new setting." In a special issue of the Gallery's *Journal*, an article called "New Installations: An Imaginary Tour" explained. With regard to the European Collection: "... the painting of walls in rich dramatic colours... recapture[s] the elegant atmosphere of the 19th-century French beaux-arts tradition." Further: "... emphasis will be placed on using the collection as a catalyst when developing ideas for... exhibitions." With regard to the Historical Canadian Collection, its galleries were "dramatically transformed, offering a rich variety of spaces, colours and textures [which] feature the most recent and most ambitious implementation of revolutionary enhancement techniques..." I learned about "the Gallery's senior exhibit interpretation team" whose "innovative work... is known internationally as being in the vanguard of interpreting art in the museum setting." So-o-o-o, these were the guys who had painted the gallery walls.

When I visited the new AGO, I favoured the new white galleries that house the Contemporary Art Collection. The Gallery, now so much bigger, was showing more of the collection than previously had been shown at one time. It took me months to locate the earlier paintings and sculptures that I think of as old friends. Often, I was disappointed to find them in dark corridors, sometimes buried in dark rooms, or blasted in bright ones.

What I saw was, at best, theatre. Each gallery was a tableau, a stage set. The paintings and sculptures played secondary, even minor, roles (as catalysts?), and I, as viewer, was unable to see in the work the presence of its own past. The gallery walls were painted with colours undreamed of (as wall paint) before the turn of the century or during the first half of this century and in every case, the wall colours interfered with the art.

What happens when the walls of a gallery are coloured? The most rudimentary understanding of light and colour will explain it. When white light (sunlight or artificial light) illuminates a coloured surface, some of the spectral rays of that light are reflected and others are absorbed. If the surface is red, the red light rays are reflected and all of the other rays are absorbed. This is how we see "red." When the walls of a gallery room have been painted red, the light (and air) in that room reddens because so much red light is reflected from the walls. This red light falls on the paintings on the walls casting a red veil over them. The colours in the paintings are altered, changed in the same way they would change if a light with a red filter were used to illuminate them. Gallery rooms painted with bright intense colours (reds, oranges and yellows) alter the colour and colour relationships in paintings shown in them.

In gallery rooms painted with dark colours (browns, dark greys, greens, blues and purples) most of the light is absorbed by the darkness of these colours. The light from each spotlight falls in a cone or a pool over the art it illuminates. There is a great contrast between the light and the surrounding darkness; it is similar to a flashlight in the dark. In a dark room, a sculpture will have black surface shadows and it will not reflect light from its surface beyond the perimeter of the pool of light; a painting's colours will alter to extreme intensities in contrasting relationship with the dark wall that surrounds it.

To see art under these conditions, the viewer stands close to the work. In a room that has brightly coloured walls, a painting has to be viewed at close range so the coloured wall will not be within one's field of vision. This does not cancel the effect the walls have on the painting, but it avoids the direct hit to the eye that the wall's colour gives when it is viewed along with the painting. In a room that has dark coloured walls, the viewer stands close to a sculpture to see its own reflected light. The viewer steps out of the darkness of the room into the pool of artificial light that illuminates the work. This light is a "hot spot," but it can not travel far; it is being absorbed by the surrounding darkness. In rooms with coloured walls, the walls' colours overwhelm the artworks, and the actual colours and forms of the art are impossible to see.

The effects I have described are observable. They are the consequence of the same phenomenon (light and colour) that surprises and engages the eye and mind in nature and in art.

In 1994, *From Cézanne to Matisse: Great French Paintings from the Barnes Foundation* was shown at the AGO. The show was promoted as a unique opportunity ("Never before. Never again.") to view some of the art collected by the eccentric Dr. Alfred Barnes. The show was well supported; advertisers' strategies and curatorial careers were staked on its success. The show could not fail; it did not. All concerned were eventually rewarded and those rewards were duly advertised as evidence of the project's success.

The exhibition hung on coloured walls in rooms constructed to simulate the appearance of the rooms at the Barnes Foundation at Merion near Philadelphia. The colours were chosen to duplicate the effect of an ochre, Dr. Barnes' favourite colour. Ochre is an earth colour, an opaque low-value yellow which can be described as a light brown. In pale tones, it behaves as a neutral colour. The walls at Merion are cloth covered; in Toronto, the "exhibit interpretation team" used paint. Paint forms a surface that reflects its colour more readily than cloth. Because cloth is textured, its ability to reflect light is reduced— even cloth of the finest weave captures some light in the interstices between its threads. To imitate cloth, the team painted two colours on some walls, sponging on or ragging off the second colour. This actually increased the coloration. Some walls were painted ochre. Never having visited Merion, I can not say how well the AGO installation evoked the experience that had been so carefully and autocratically controlled by Dr. Barnes, but I suspect that the team overshot the mark.

The intensity of the yellow-orange walls in the first two rooms of the exhibit had a damaging effect on the paintings of Auguste Renoir. The wall colour heightened the colours of faces and figures in the paintings and it lowered and intensified the blues and blue-purples in them. The coloured walls altered the relationships in the paintings. It is not surprising that the Renoir paintings were panned by the press and disliked by many artists and members of the public.

One person, Nancy Hazelgrove, recognized the problem and in a letter that appeared in *The Globe and Mail* (October 13, 1994) described it as follows:

> A basic phenomenon of colour contrast occurs by placing relatively small paintings in the first two rooms on expanses of turgid yellow walls. Simultaneous contrast is activated, accentuating the violet-purple range within the painting and dulling the other colours. When the walls change to a more neutral colour in the

> last two rooms, it is again possible to see the work without as strong a subliminal colour influence.
>
> The first priority toward masterpieces is to preserve their integrity by placing them [on] a neutral ground. By appropriating them into a grand design, a decorative environment, neither the public nor the artworks is well served. Why doesn't the AGO know this?

Hazelgrove is a knowledgeable observer; her account is accurate. Her concern for the integrity of the art raises the question of curatorial responsibility. A week later, *The Globe and Mail* published a letter from Shirley Kofman that responded to Hazelgrove's letter:

> This is not a valid criticism. The AGO's first priority in this show is to duplicate, as closely as possible, the Barnes Foundation's display in Philadelphia.

Kofman supported her statement by quoting a passage from the AGO's *Journal* (Volume 2, Number 5, September-October 1994, page 11): "To evoke the classic proportions of the Barnes Foundation's galleries, special ceiling mouldings and baseboards have been designed, as well as other touches, including the use of Dr. Barnes' favourite ochre colour on some walls in the heart of the installation. [...] We have paid special attention [...] using special painting techniques that suggest the cloth covered walls at the Barnes Foundation. [...]"

This passage doesn't convince me, as it did Kofman, that the AGO's interpretation team was trying to *duplicate* the Barnes Foundation; rather, its stated aim was to *evoke* it. As I said above, the colours were chosen to duplicate the *effect* of ochre. Hazelgrove noticed as I did (and at the expense of Renoir, so did others) where the shot went wild. But the team had more than this on its collective mind. From the same issue of the *Journal*: "Given the size and flexibility of the... Zacks Pavilion, the Gallery has had the opportunity to create an installation that is consciously different from those in Washington, Paris, Tokyo and Fort Worth." And one of the team added: "... we are choreographing the visit and creating a variety of moods. Our installation will be very dramatic."

The letters written by Nancy Hazelgrove and Shirley Kofman represent two opposing views about the museum's role in our time. Hazelgrove believes that artworks have integrity which is to be preserved (not interfered with). This view gives the Gallery and its curators the role of custodians, keepers of those things that we value as art, as history and as culture. Access to these things by the public is possible only when their authenticity is respected. Kofman, on the other hand, favours the current project to use art as stagecraft to evoke a time or place. This view gives the Gallery and its curators license to revise, to interpret, and thereby *renew* art, or make the art of other times relevant to current thought. This, according to the theory, makes art more accessible. And what about the members of the exhibit interpretation team? Well— they seem to be giving us a song and a dance.

What is a neutral colour? The word "neutral" describes a colour that has little or no influence on other colours. Grey is a neutral colour, but to behave as background for art, it must be a light grey. Light grey paints lean toward a colour (blue-grey, or the "warm" greys which lean to red and yellow). Often, neutral walls are cloth-covered; their colours, like the ochre described above, are light brown or beige, and we refer to them as "natural" colours. However, any colour will function as a neutral background if it is pale enough; such colours are called "off-whites." White is the most "neutral" colour of all.

What happens when a gallery's walls are white? All of the white light that illuminates the room is reflected as white light from the walls; that is, its spectral rays do not separate; the light that is absorbed is minimal. White light is reflected from wall to wall and this light, as well as the light from the source of illumination, illuminates the art in the room. Paintings and sculptures in the room reflect and absorb this light according to their colours and surfaces. The room seems larger. The air is lighter because white light is moving and being reflected from every white surface. Only the objects in the room reflect colour and this colour travels; it can be seen from yards, sometimes whole rooms away. In a gallery with white walls, it is possible to examine a work closely as well as view it from a distance. Paintings report their colours for great distances. Sculptures reflect ambient light from every side; there are no black shadows on them— the shadows are grey. One sees a painting's actual colour and its colour relationships are not impaired. One sees a sculpture's actual surface and form. Is it any wonder that this experience is preferred?

Last year, I saw *Barbara Hepworth: A Retrospective*, the first show of Hepworth's work since 1968. In it, all periods of Hepworth's work, from 1927 to her death in 1975, were represented. On the way to Toronto, my friend and driver, Nelson, asked me, "Will the Hepworth show have coloured walls?" Believing that the AGO curators had some intelligence, I said, "No. Hepworth is a modernist; her work is about light. Don't worry, the walls will be white."

When we entered the Zacks Pavilion, I saw dark grey walls. The room was dotted with Hepworth's early sculptures; each piece was isolated in a hot pool from a spotlight and all were separated by darkness. I set aside my disappointment and looked at everything.

It was difficult. The lighting in the darkness of the room was harsh. It caused the shadows that each sculpture casts upon itself to be hard and black. In a room with white walls, those shadows would be soft and grey. They would gather in some light, reflect it back to the viewer whose eyes then would follow the form of the surface of the work. As it was, the high contrast between the lighting and the surrounding darkness made surface shadows so dark that they cut into the surfaces like black holes. I was puzzled by what seemed to be incised double lines on some works. With my fingers, I explored the edge of the clear plastic case that covered one of them and discovered (by seeing the shadow of my hand on the sculpture) that the double lines were the shadow of the joined edge of the plastic case. In a room with white walls, ambient light would dissolve this kind of shadow. All of the shadows interrupted the actual forms of the sculptures. But the lighting (and darkness) had a further effect on the works. The marble and alabaster looked like soap. By nature, these materials are translucent— light passes through them. Without the condition of moving light, they lost their luminosity; here, they were as dense as plaster.

Drawings were displayed in another room on walls that were painted dark blue— I mean dark, dark blue. The works could not report beyond the perimeter of the cone of light cast on them. Because so much light was being absorbed by the walls, the drawings seemed weak in the darkness of the room. I watched people try to look at them. They were standing within inches of the drawings. In an adjoining room, a film made during Hepworth's retrospective at the Tate in 1968 was being shown. It was narrated by Hepworth. I watched it and heard her talk about her work, about light on it and in it. Hepworth favoured showing her sculptures outside in daylight.

The last rooms were painted a lighter grey than the grey in the first rooms. (Or did it only seen lighter after the darkness of the blue?) I felt relieved when I entered, but soon lost the sense of light. Hepworth's *Torso*, a familiar work from the AGO's permanent collection, suffered from the lack of light; the colour and texture of its surface were lost. It stood near a wall. Only the front was illuminated; the back was lost in shadow. In a room with white walls, the back of this work would be lightened by the ambient light reflected from the wall. Hepworth's late works were in the final room. This was my chance to see where Hepworth had taken her work in the last years of her life. Here were Hepworth's perfect marble spheres; here, they were as opaque as bowling balls.

When I met Nelson again outside the Pavilion, I said, "I was wrong." He summed it up with this succinct, minimalist thought: "They're nuts."

Barbara Hepworth lived and worked at St. Ives in Cornwall, England, where the light is remarkable. St. Ives is on a peninsula where the sunlight is reflected from the water on both sides of the land. In no way is it reasonable to install the Hepworth retrospective in rooms with dark coloured walls. Knowledge of the work and of the period makes the idea absurd. Am I to believe that the installation was meant to evoke a time and place? What time; what place? The "atmosphere" should have been one of light and air, and that could have been accomplished merely by painting the walls white. Did the exhibit interpretation team think the installation enhanced the work? Was it "drama" that the team was after? If so, the team should have watched the opening minutes of the 1968 film to hear Hepworth's thoughts on that matter. Was the team intent on making this installation "consciously different" from the exhibition's last venue? Did the installation renew Hepworth's work in some way? If "installation" is equal to "interpretation," what were the curators saying?

I believe the installation prevented access to Hepworth's works as surely as if the curators had turned off the lights and locked the doors. What they did shows a lack of knowledge about the artist, the work, the period, and about the *modernist imperative* in art. Have the curators been blinded by their own version of a post-modern theory that gives unbridled authority to the (mis)interpretation and (mis)representation of art? Post-modern theory is rife with rhetoric (and brackets). The Hepworth installation shows, not only a lack, but a *loss* of knowledge, and that deeply disturbs me. How we see what we see is knowledge hard-won; its history spans the millennium.

The Greeks thought that vision resulted from light rays emitted from the eyes to an object. This idea prevailed until AD 1000 when the Arabian mathematician, Alhazen, understood for the first time that vision was the result of light rays reflected from an object into the eyes. First artists (the cone of light from object to eye informs perspective), then scientists (Newton's *Optics*) advanced knowledge by the method that art and science share— observation. In the 19th and 20th centuries, art and science achieved a new consciousness of vision and light. The art of this period is modernist and its most stringent practice was in the first part of this century. Modernist art informs all art today, and in art museums, we have the opportunity to see it, to study it, and to understand it. To do this, it is essential that we see it unimpeded by pretentious decor; that is, it should be seen as it was seen by the artist *in the artist's studio*. (The artist is the first viewer of his own work. The collector and the curator are late-comers to any work of art.)

However, among curators and critics there are post-modern theorists who are borrowing ideas from modern science and using them for their own purposes. For instance, the Principle of Uncertainty in physics, which describes knowledge as limited, is translated in literary criticism to an "indeterminacy" that in art criticism becomes an *absolute* which says that art has no inherent meaning or integrity. Art, then, is given meaning by "interpretation." As the AGO advertised: "You are invited to reflect, ponder, debate. There are no right answers. There is only your interpretation." This thinking has the effect of metaphorically reversing the understanding of the cone of light. It ignores the phenomena of light, colour and vision and implies that because knowledge is limited, there is no use for it at all. This does not inform; it misleads. It gives the authority (authorship) of art to everyone *except* the artist who made it. By showing art in rooms with coloured walls, there is little chance that the public will notice what they are missing. In Russia, we have learned, modernist art was hidden in vaults so the people could not see it; here, curators are accomplishing the same thing by burying it in rooms with coloured walls.

In 1995, the National Gallery in Ottawa opened *The Group of Seven: Art for a Nation*. The show was assembled by Charles Hill, curator of Canadian Art at that Gallery. The exhibit was structured by the Group's first eight exhibitions held at the Art Gallery of Toronto (AGO) between 1920 and 1931. Hill wished to show by the paintings of the group members and their contemporaries that these artists had taken an "anti-academic stance... It was a modernist movement within the terms of modernism in Canada..." Of Hill's thesis, Robert Fulford, in *Canadian Art* (Fall 1995), wrote, "Hill wants to remind us how radical the Group was then... He wants to recover the Group's legitimacy as an avant-garde and place it once again in the stream of Modernism."

I didn't see the show in Ottawa; I planned to see it in Toronto. It opened at the AGO in February 1996. But the AGO used Hill's show as a catalyst for an examination of nationhood and identity called *The OH! Canada Project*. Additional exhibits included six community arts groups and six school groups, and a number of interactive programs. The AGO's *Journal* (January-February, 1996) promised, "... a variety of innovative, related activities will both inform and entertain." Director Maxwell Anderson: "*The OH! Canada Project* is an example of how the... Gallery... is developing integrated presentations designed to bring art and people together in fresh and relevant ways." And what about Hill's Group of Seven painters exhibit? Chief curator Matthew Teitelbaum: "*Art for a Nation* is an exciting opportunity to re-examine the relevance of the paintings of the Group of Seven." S-s-s-slight change, that, from what Charles Hill intended.

I followed the progress of *The OH! Canada Project* as news and in reviews and commentaries (they were mixed). My interest centred on Charles Hill's exhibit and I was curious about the adjunct shows and activities. It would be difficult for me to see *The OH! Canada Project*— it takes several visits to see so large an exhibition. The winter was long, cold and stormy; my plans to visit the Gallery were postponed over and over again.

One evening, the TV news had a brief item on *The OH! Canada Project*. (I have a small screen, black and white television set.) For a few seconds there was a shot of a viewer looking at a painting reported to be by "the-group-of-seven." A woman, only inches away from the painting, was standing inside the cone of illumination from an overhead light, surrounded by *blackness*. From this, I knew that the gallery walls were coloured, and in that room, the colour was very dark. In that moment I knew that I no longer wanted to see the exhibition because all of the colour relationships in the paintings would be altered by the colour of the walls. Access denied. I let the show go by.

What colour were the walls at the National Gallery in Ottawa when the exhibition was there? I don't know. What colour were the walls at the AGO? This "detail" was not mentioned in the promotion for the show, in any of the reviews I read, or in the commentaries I heard. I learned later that each gallery room for *The Group of Seven: Art for a Nation* was painted a different colour— green was mentioned to me as the dark colour I saw on my television screen. But the question that is most *relevant* is: What colour were the gallery walls at the AGO from 1920 to 1931; that is, what colour were they over the period of the eight exhibitions of the work by these Canadian painters being (mis)(re)presented again at the AGO in the *OH! Canada* show? I think I know the answer; they were neutral.

I believe that 19th- and 20th-century art, in particular, should not be displayed in rooms with coloured walls. I believe art of every period should be displayed in rooms with white or neutral walls *to preserve the integrity of the work and make it clearly accessible to all who wish to know it*.

In theory, coloured walls in art museums help "to close the gap between art and the people." This sounds like an admirable goal, but it is impossible to achieve this way. Two things prevent it. First, with coloured walls, the curators are adding, in effect, another colour (a big swatch of it— the wall) to every painting in the room destroying the integrity, the actual appearance, of each work. Second, the "interpretation" of the already distorted art is thrown open to speculation based on either a lack of knowledge or on knowledge that is being withheld by the same curators who profess to have it.

The curators need to stop the rhetoric and return the walls to white (light). This will close the so-called gap between art and the people. The art will be returned to the artist, its rightful author, and every viewer will have an equal chance to see it.

11 November, 1996

Writings About My Work (1973-2000)

Telling About Line Telling.

Art does not reproduce the visible; it makes visible.

Paul Klee. *Creative Credo.*

Line is measure.

Paul Klee. *On Modern Art.*

Line is measure. It is measured. It measures. It measures the page. It measures time and energy.

The size/shape of the page is the first decision. The activity goes on within. Even if the drawing suggests activity beyond the page, it is not there. It is on the page. The act that makes the first mark, its energy is recorded there. That mark incites. The whole page is activated by it. Draw a line, the space of the page is interrupted by it, acting with and against it and a dialogue begins. Continue the dialogue. The completed drawing is that dialogue.

That is what making pictures is. I write about it— "about" as if around— because what it is is the picture. It tells itself. These words are another drawing. They form lines. They measure the page. You can measure this line.

There are no lines in nature. Cézanne said that and many people have said it over again. I say it to point out that the page is autonomous, the line is autonomous and so is the drawing whether it is a drawing of no thing or a picture of something. When the drawing is a picture of something, it tells of that thing and it tells of its making.

A picture of something— say, a house— may involve the illusion of perspective. Perspective is not a thing of the house nor a thing of the drawing. It is a thing of the eye and the place where a person is standing to look at a house. Correct perspective is a device that assumes a viewer has one eye and does not move his head. If the viewer moves, the perspective changes. A drawing of a house will have lines that converge, that move up and across, and down and across the page. Lines that draw a picture of something and lines that make a drawing of no thing are the same in their autonomy.

The character of line is told by Paul Klee in *The Thinking Eye*. What Klee knows is set down there for everyone. I will tell here how I make my drawings.

The drawings in the first series were made with stencils. I made the stencils by cutting the shapes I wanted from card— square shapes and some irregular shapes related to the square. In the beginning I used combinations of these shapes, but as the work went on I used fewer and fewer irregular shapes until the drawings were built from the square shape alone. I made 40 drawings. The size of the page was 18" x 24". I placed the stencil on the page and drew lines within the opening moving the graphite pencil diagonally from top right to bottom left. [I am left-handed.] I moved the stencil to draw the next shape, drew again— the same process— until the page was packed and stacked with the drawn shapes. The drawing came together as a unit and each of its units was a drawing.

Each shape was drawn with one continuing line. Drawing diagonally from top right to bottom left— short lines to long lines to short lines again— created a change in tone. Where the lines were shortest they were darkest. This variation, one of energy change, occurred whether I used a soft pencil or a hard one. I changed pencil weight from drawing to drawing and within drawings. Sometimes I overlapped the shapes at their edges. Where the lines overlapped they were darkest. Sometimes I left a white space between the drawn shapes. The shapes, ordered as if on a horizontal/vertical grid, stagger inside and sometimes off that grid.

That is how I made the second series of drawings. They are on a 22" x 29" page. I used only the square stencil. The stencil openings were 1" square, 2" square and 2 1/2" square. Using the 1" square stencil, I made four drawings essentially the same, exploring the samenesses and differences that occurred in each drawing. Each drawing was a new event. I went on to use each stencil size in drawings and I combined the sizes. I made another

40 drawings. I made drawings for about two months and it was as if I did nothing else in that time. The process is slow. It must be sustained. *Series 1* and *Series 2* were each made over two-month-long periods about six months apart.

The next work was made with the stencils, but I drew only one ruled line for each square shape. That line, ruled from top left to bottom right, described the square by one of its diagonals. On a large page, I packed and stacked the squares, drawing each one's diagonal in the same direction. These drawings are difficult to "see." They depend on the simultaneous reaction of the viewer's eye. The diagonals, by their positions, their relationship to each other and their relationship to the order of the overall composition, invite the square to become visible. One sees the drawn diagonals, then the square shapes appear as grey shapes separated by spaces that glow white. This occurs by the simultaneous reaction of the eye. Only the ruled lines are in fact on the page. These works need time to be seen. Some viewers are slow to experience the reaction. To my eye the effect is immediate. Others experience no simultaneous reaction at all. Making these drawings was slow and tedious work. The act of drawing did not flow like it did with the earlier work. The whole drawing is an event. Making it was labour. Each unit is an oblique on the page. When all are collected the square shapes emerge.

In *Series 4* the square is a contour, drawn deliberately, unruled, its four sides having the irregularities of a free-hand motion. The page is 15" x 15". The squares are drawn with 1 2 3 4 lines, then the next, then the next. That activity was sustained until the page was filled with shapes that varied as each one found its place and shape by the last one drawn. Each drawing insisted on another new drawing. I made 45 drawings. I consider 29 of them successful works. The shapes and the spaces between the shapes are regular in some drawings, irregular in others. Where the shapes are regular and the spaces irregular, the shapes are dominant. Where the shapes are very small and regular, the spaces between the shapes are dominant even when the spaces are irregular. Where the spaces between the shapes are regular, it is as if a web has been drawn. In some drawings where the shapes are pressed to irregularities, a linear flow up/down and across occurs. Throughout all of this work I was essentially making the same drawing over and over again. Each new page was the beginning of a new event. Each drawing completed was a new event. Making each drawing was a different experience from the last, so each drawing is different.

The horizontal/vertical order in each drawing is an element separate from the drawn unit shapes. A grid is not drawn but its appearance occurs when all of the units have been drawn. The unit square is not in fact a square, but it has the order and energy of a square whether drawn by a continuing diagonal line as in *Series 1* and *Series 2* or by a contour line in *Series 4*. The horizontal/vertical is a relationship of greatest linear opposition. The samenesses of the spaces formed at the intersection of the two linear directions is the antithesis of that opposition. My drawings are not made by ordered calculation but in their making they answer to it.

All of the drawings were made with graphite pencils. That medium responds to the pressure of the hand making darker and lighter lines. Even when I attempted to maintain an even pressure, variations in tone occurred. The body tires, the hand tires, the mind tires and the line will tell of this. The pencil yields.

This is the thing of drawing. The action, the event, the making and the seeing. The completed drawing viewed is a new event. Each viewing is a new experience different from the last for the person who has made the drawing and for the viewer with another eye.

1973

Paintings 1969-1977.

> Intuition enlightens and so links up with pure thought. They together become an intelligence which is not simply of the brain, which does not calculate, but which feels and thinks. Which is creative both in art and life. From this intelligence there must arise non-figurative art in which instinct no longer plays a dominating part. Those who do not understand this intelligence regard non-figurative art as a purely intellectual product.
>
> Piet Mondrian[1]

Intuition, the immediate apprehension by the mind without reasoning, must not be confused with instinct. Instinct is innate skill and it does not link with thought.

The separation of intuition and intelligence accounts for the idea that artists produce art either by instinct or by calculation. The nature of thought forbids so rigid a separation. One thinks, one reasons, one understands, but understanding need not occur by this process alone; it may occur by intuition. The intellect is exercised by thought and reason; the experience of enlightenment by intuition startles the intellect, opening it to new passages of thought.

Mondrian refutes the idea that non-figurative art is calculated. Calculation does not enter into the experience. This can be seen when the part played by intuition is acknowledged. Mondrian describes an intelligence that is not simply of the brain; it *feels and thinks*. It is this intelligence that I speak of in relation to my art. I point to Mondrian for precedent, not to impress the reader with my intelligence, but to remind him that I am not without feeling.

I want to get at something basic in my work. By writing about it, I will be confined to a process that is linear, word after word. So linear a process conflicts with the idea about which I wish to write. The experience I will write about is visual, a thing seen, and that seeing may occur in a moment. Seeing-in-a-moment is like the immediate apprehension by intuition. It is perception.

Words like "truth" and "beauty" have passed from the vocabulary of art. The idea of the spiritual has followed. It is a pity that words like these have lost their meaning because they answer to a common human experience. Insight by intuition is an experience like the one we would have called "spiritual" in an earlier time. That insight might have been "truth," and that truth, "beauty." Artists are still making beautiful things. Artists still feel a sense of enlightenment in what they achieve and are pressed on by it in their search for another or a new visual experience, but we use other words to tell of it now. Some words seem "intellectual," and the artist and his art are placed on the side of *pure intellect*. The artist who says nothing, or is inarticulate, is placed on the side of *pure emotion*. Neither artist is without intellect or emotion.

My paintings are about colour. Colour is a visual experience. A colour work must be seen. Colour means something. It is itself: that is what it means. The variety of colour experience cannot be described.

We seldom question colour as a visual fact. We think of it most often in relation to something else and believe that we are thinking of colour. *Colour* is different from "a coloured thing." Although all things have colour, colour is a phenomenon apart from any thing. It is this phenomenon that I am concerned with in my work.

It is colour phenomena that interest me, not colour theory. For an artist, colour theories are important; they are tools for his work. Theories analyze colour; they are a knowledge that an artist must have, but in his study of theories he will discover their limitations. A study of colour theories gives an understanding of how colour works, how the eye works, how the eye sees colour, but it does not account for all the phenomena of colour. It does not account for that experience of colour which, like intuition, enlightens and startles the mind.

A painting is a thing of paint and that fact cannot be ignored. The experience of colour in a painting is achieved by paint or pigment, and that tool limits the work. The limits of colour painting, however, have not been reached in the hundreds of years that artists have been painting. Artists have always used colour, but its use as a dominant element in painting is a recent development in art. I believe it is also a recent development in perception, and so it has no conceivable limit. We know more about colour, we see more in colour, and colour theories tell us more about colour than earlier. All processes go on and will continue to go on.

When I speak of colour energy, I mean the *presence* of colour. Each colour exerts an energy that excites the eye and mind. Combinations of colours create an activity between them, a play of their energies that itself creates a new energy. Combining more colours creates more energies to excite the eye and mind. Combinations of energies create excitations, distinct and various, and this experience opens new perceptions.

Particular colours may invite particular responses. A particular combination of colours may invite another particular response. Kandinsky, in *Concerning the Spiritual in Art*, tries to account for a particular response generated by the combination of an intense red with an intense blue. There is a particular excitation created by this combination that is easily distinguished from any other colour pair. Both red and blue are primary colours. The other primary, yellow, although a distinct contrast to either red or blue, does not create the same or even similar excitation. Yellow excites a sensation too like red when combined with it, or too different from blue when combined with it. The red/blue pair create a unique excitation. Kandinsky describes colour in terms of his own sensibilities. He uses words that describe emotions and he attributes these emotional responses to the colours. I prefer to avoid this means of description. I believe it leads the senses. I prefer that colour lead, and lead wherever perception is capable of going.

Line and shape are planar tools. A line can be a line and it can make a [contour] shape. A shape can be *full of colour*, and so becomes a colour-shape. A shape that can be described as a thing or by geometry, can be filled with colour, and so becomes a colour*ed* shape. A colour*ed* shape is perceived differently than is a colour-shape. A colour*ed* shape is named, then coloured; a colour-shape is named by its colour. Colour and shape cannot be seen separately; colour takes shape, or a shape is coloured. If a shape is coloured, the shape will dominate. When colour takes shape, it dominates the shape. I call that *colour-shape*.

A colour-shape occupies an area. The colour energy of that shape directs, or is active on the plane. If the colour-shape is like a square, that is, if it has the order and energy of a square even though it is not a square, it will be a still shape, without direction. If the colour-shape is wider than high, its direction will be horizontal. If it is a tall shape, its direction will be vertical. The energy of the shape, its direction or lack of it, melds with the colour of that shape and becomes an active part of the combinations of energies that excite the eye and mind, and it increases the various excitations.

A shape is sometimes defined by another shape. When we refer to "positive and negative space," we mean that the shape of a thing or a geometric shape is positive and the shape of the space that surrounds the first shape is negative. Making a positive shape can make all else negative. Making many positive shapes increases the positive aspect. Making many colour-shapes can invite the eye to select some of those shapes as positive and others as negative. Josef Albers has said that any colour can be made to appear to be positive or negative. Vasarely has said that when a colour is repeated, that colour will become negative. If more than one colour is repeated, any colour can be positive while all others are negative, or any two, or any three colours, and so on until all the colours can be seen as positive. This is what Guido Molinari has done with his colour verticals. In Molinari's paintings, the eye can enter anywhere.

In my Colour Lock paintings, all of the colour-shapes are positive. I put colour-shape beside colour-shape and so fill up the canvas. No colour-shape touches the next, so no shape is defined by the next. Each colour-shape is a positive gesture, both on the canvas and in its making. Because no colour-shape touches the next, the canvas is visible between each colour-shape and at the painting's edge. The activity of the painting is *on the canvas surface*; it is made that way and it is seen that way. Each colour-shape has a place to act out its energies.

"Canvas visible," or raw-canvas-showing, is another planar tool. In Frank Stella's paintings, a narrow line of canvas alternates with each colour.

In this way, Stella stabilizes the picture plane. The eye does not make positive/negative choices; the illusion of advancing and receding colours is interfered with. While certain colours are believed to advance in any situation, recession is fully stopped. No colour will recede because of the visible canvas surface. The advance of a yellow shape, for instance, is slowed down because the yellow can *expand into the canvas space*. The energy of the yellow is moving in two directions and the appearance that it is advancing is impaired.

The visible canvas in my Colour Lock paintings behaves in this manner. It gives each colour the opportunity to flex or to occupy a space larger than itself. The combinations of colour-shapes act out their energies in comfort, both for the colours and for the eye that perceives them.

I have used the series title, *Colour Lock*, for my paintings since 1970. The word “Lock” refers to the interaction of the colour energies which come together as a *wholeness* in a completed painting. The idea of wholeness is an important one to me; it seems to be the point at which one begins, and the place at which one stops. This sounds as if there is nothing in between; in fact, the whole event of making a painting is between *that* start and *that* stop. In Paul Klee’s words, “Art makes visible.” One paints to make visible. I paint what I want to see. I paint it so I can see it. I start with some intelligence of what I am about, and I bring that into being with paint and canvas. Only then can I have *found out* the painting.

There is *wonder* in colour; it is like a romance. The orchestra of visual sensations in the activity of colour energies creates an excitation that surprises the eye and mind. This may be similar to the uplifting experience of spiritual love. Paul Klee’s diary entry (Kairouan, April 16, 1914) reads:

> Colour has me. I no longer need reach for it. It has me forever and knows it. That is the meaning of this happy hour. Colour and I are one. I am a painter.

Klee uses an emotional language to describe his insight. The freshness of the experience may have moved him to write this romantic passage. First plateaus in perceptual gains seem the most dramatic. New gains of insight, even greater gains, will seem less overwhelming because they are added to an already conscious awareness.

My first Colour Lock paintings seemed to me to be a tremendous breakthrough. In my earlier paintings I had used low value colour: blue-grey, green-grey, purple-grey and black. My search for form and order in these works is somehow like cubist paintings insofar as analytical cubism was carried through without involving high colour. Frank Stella's earliest paintings were black and in them, he established a form and order into which he later brought colour. My paintings prior to the Colour Lock paintings are important to me. I was totally involved in them and did not notice my lack of commitment to colour. But I remember the great leap into colour with the Colour Lock paintings and I understand Paul Klee's diary entry of 1914.

6 April, 1977

Note:

1. Piet Mondrian. "Plastic Art and Pure Plastic Art (Figurative and Non-Figurative Art)" in *Circle*, 1937.

The Colour Lock Paintings 1969-1983.

My first Colour Lock paintings were a tremendous breakthrough for me. In my earlier paintings (1968-9), I had used low value colour: blue-grey, green-grey, purple-grey and black. Shape and form, order and organization were my dominant concerns. The energy of shape, order and direction took precedence over colour, and the low value colour gave place to the graphic elements. I remember the great leap into colour with the Colour Lock paintings.

It will be difficult to write about the Colour Lock paintings. They span 15 years. As paintings, each is its own history; as 15 years of work, they show my search for colour, its language, its vocabulary and its meaning. I believe that painting is event; I believe that colour is event; I believe that that event is meaning.

The Colour Lock paintings are serial. There have been nine separate series of paintings. I did not set out in 1969 to make nine series of paintings; I didn't even set out to make one. Rather, I made one painting that gave colour and its energy precedence over the graphic elements of the work, and then, I made another. The second painting confirmed the first. A third painting confirmed and clarified both and revealed a new event which demanded of me another painting. Seriality evolved. It is a searching process that allows me to explore the avenue of thought that motivates a painting, and that which is revealed by the completed work. Each painting is an event in the making of it and another event in the seeing of it.

Whatever idea motivates the making of a painting, whether emotional or rational, the act of making, that event, overtakes the idea that initiated the act. The stuff of the mind is not the stuff of paint. Ideas cannot be rendered in paint. Ideas are seeds that germinate into actions. When the action is the act of painting, the idea is displaced by the event of making. The painter must make it (the painting) to see it (the event). The making is the act of creating; the seeing is perception.

Throughout the Colour Lock paintings, I have worked with intense colour, with colour as "black," colour as "grey" and colour as "white." I have worked with colour-shapes on the natural canvas ground and on a coloured ground. I have worked with order and direction as an adjunct to colour which modifies and is modified by colour.

Colour and shape are not perceived separately in a painting. As concepts, colour and shape can be separated and analyzed, but as visual experience, as event, they are perceived together as one thing. I use the word "colour-shape" to describe the components of my paintings. Each colour-shape has a hue, a value and intensity, and it has size, shape and direction. The colour-shapes act *on* the natural canvas or *on* a coloured ground. In the Colour Lock paintings, colour is the more active element of the colour-shapes.

In the Colour Lock paintings, the *size* of the colour-shapes has been *large* rather than *small*. In each series of paintings, the size of the colour-shapes has been *like*. In each painting, the size of the colour-shapes is sometimes *the same*, or equivalent, and all are sufficiently large to prohibit competition and strong contrasts in size.

The *shape* of the colour-shapes in all of the paintings has been still and orderly: square-like and rectangular loose-edged shapes. The *direction* of the colour-shapes has been most often *none*. Just as a point can be said to have no direction, so a square-like shape can be said to have no direction. Where a rectangular shape occurs in my paintings, I consider that rectangle to be the extension of a square; that is, a horizontal shape is a square extended to the left or right, and a vertical shape is a square extended upward or downward. The still shape has become active without loss of order. It is a new shape and it has *direction*. Just as a point becomes line when it moves in any direction, so the still square-like shape extended transforms its energy into activity, and the new shape declares that activity and can be said to have direction.

However, a square is not a point. The square is a still shape and it has a particular order and energy. Consider the square from the inside. It can be described as a point from which two equal co-ordinates, horizontal and vertical, extend. Add to these two more co-ordinates extended equally at

45 degrees from the first two. The relationship of the second pair to the first pair of lines is the same as that of the hypotenuse of a right-triangle to its other two sides. Now consider the square as the *frame* of the energy of either or both pairs of co-ordinates of the point. It is this view of shape that occurs in my paintings. In the Colour Lock paintings, I consider the square-like shape as a point filled up and filled out with *colour*.

The concept "colour" is different from the perception of colour. Colour is a visual experience, a perceived reality new to the eye and mind when it is encountered, and new again on each subsequent encounter.

Colour is phenomenon. When that phenomenon is examined, a theory is formulated. A theory is a supposition explaining something and it may be based on principles independent of the phenomenon. Colour theories supply a structure and a system which account for some part of the event of colour. They supply a vocabulary for colour and some part of the experience of colour. Colour theories conceptualize perceptual experience. When colour theories are confused with colour experience, colour is believed to be a concept and the perception of colour is prejudiced and impaired. For a painter, a study of colour theories is useful and important, but the painter's eye and mind are his most important tools. He must be conscious of colour; he must notice it. Perception can be said to be simply *noticing*.

To see colour, three things are necessary: 1) a coloured thing, 2) light, 3) the eye. The word "colour" can mean a particular hue, any combination of hues, and all hues separately and together; it can mean all of the spectral rays, separately and in any combination, and implied by the word "colour" is the sensation on the eye by rays of decomposed light. That sensation (recept) and the consciousness of the mind (percept) of the spectral rays reflected from a coloured thing, all this is implicit in the word (concept) "colour."

1) A coloured thing.

All things can be said to have colour. In painting, colour is pigment, and pigment is matter. Theories that examine and explain the behaviour of coloured matter involve *subtractive* mixture. These theories isolate three primary colours: red, yellow and blue. Intermixtures of two primary colours yield the secondary colours: orange, green and purple. The relationship of each secondary colour to the remaining or excluded primary colour is said to be complementary, that is, the secondary colour *completes* that primary colour. Intermixtures of secondary colours with the remaining primary yield black. The principle of *subtractive* mixture, simply stated, is that all intermixtures of pigments yield a new colour that proceeds toward black; that is, reflected rays of light are progressively excluded and absorbed until no light is reflected and the intermixture yields black. When red, yellow and blue are intermixed, they yield *black*.[1]

2) Light.

Light illuminates and makes visible a coloured thing. Light rays are reflected and absorbed by the coloured thing. Theories that examine and explain the behaviour of light involve *additive* colour. These theories describe the behaviour of the colours of the spectrum. When white light is passed through a prism, it refracts and divides into the spectrum. The colours of the spectrum are generally described by five colour names: red, yellow, green, blue and violet. When one colour ray is separated from the rest and the remaining rays are collected together, they yield the complement of the separated colour ray. When all the rays are collected together, they yield white light. The principle of *additive* colour, simply stated, is that when some light rays are reflected from a coloured thing and other rays are absorbed by it, the colour of that thing is made visible. When all the rays are absorbed by a thing, that thing is black; when all the rays are reflected, that thing is white.

3) The eye.

The eye is moving all the time, or, it moves and rests and moves again. Colour receptors in the eye are stimulated by light rays. When the light ray is a spectral ray reflected from a coloured thing, a colour sensation occurs. This sensation generates impulses which pass to the brain and colour perception takes place.

Perception, then, involves the brain or mind. When colour is perceived, the mind is activated and the intellect is engaged, and so the emotions are aroused. It is through this process that we see colour, that we know that we are seeing it, that we say that we *respond* to colour. For a colour event to occur, two things must happen in nature and two things must happen in the observer; in nature: the phenomenon of coloured matter and the phenomenon of light; in the observer: the activity of the eye and the activity of the mind.

A simple experiment will illustrate. A red colour chip is placed on a sheet of white paper. An observer is asked to focus on the red chip for several seconds, then the red chip is removed. The observer, now focusing on the white paper, will see a filmic "green" shape appear where the red chip had been. This is called a successive reaction of the eye. Red and green are complementary colours.

What made a green shape appear when the red chip was removed? While the observer's eye was focused on the red chip, it became saturated by the red light rays reflected from the chip. When the red chip was removed, white light was reflected from the paper and the observer's eye was filled with white light. But the observer's eye is fatigued, saturated with red light rays, and is no longer receptive to them. It is as if the observer's eye rejects the red light rays and accepts all the rest. When red light rays are separated from the spectrum and the remaining rays collected, they yield the complement of red, "green."

The observer's eye, saturated and fatigued, required equilibrium, or rest; it divided the white light to satisfy its need. This reaction of the eye can also occur simultaneously; that is, while the red chip is in place on the white paper and being focused upon, the observer will see green appear at the outer boundary of the chip where it meets the white paper.

I have noticed when I have been teaching about colour that in every case where simultaneous and successive reactions were tested and demonstrated, the observer also reacted with marked excitement or laughter. Even when an informed observer who knows in advance what the reaction will be tests his eye, he smiles to himself when it occurs. I believe that the observers' expressions of excitement and satisfaction are significant. The eye requires, and seeks, equilibrium. The mechanism of the eye is able to satisfy its need. The observer's mind reports the eye's equilibrium and the observer expresses his pleasure. Colour, consciously observed, excites and satisfies the eye and mind.

It was the experience of making the Colour Lock paintings that made me aware of the *interdependence* of colour. Each primary colour is dependent on each other primary colour. Coloured matter, or pigment, is organic or of mineral origin. Pigment occurs naturally or it is artificially prepared. Coloured matter is *of the earth*, whether it has been mined from the earth or found on the surface. It can be said to be of the darkness of the earth in its primal state. Matter's primal colour is black. This primal black divides into the primary colours of matter: red, yellow and blue. Just as white light divides into the five spectral rays which, when collected, return again to white light, so out of the primal black come the three primary colours, and when they are intermixed, they yield black again. White light issues from the sun and is the primal colour of the sun (white). Pigment issues from the earth and is the primal colour of the earth (black). I do not say this to make poetry, but to point to the order of nature.

All painters work with colour, but a colour painter makes colour work. Colour painting is about colour, its energy and activity, its interaction and interdependence. Every aspect of colour is important; every colour and every nuance of every colour must be noticed. When colour is consciously perceived, the observer names it, remarks upon it, wants to communicate the experience to another individual. Whether he is a painter or the viewer of a painting, he will need words to speak of the event. He needs a system, or a *science*.

The Beginnings of the Science of Art.

I quote these passages from Wassily Kandinsky's *Point and Line to Plane*, which was originally published in 1926.

> Painting... has attained a level which imperiously demands that an exact scientific examination be made about the pictorial means and purpose of painting. Without such an investigation, further advance is impossible— either for the artist or the general public.

> It can be assumed with complete certainty that painting was not always lacking in theory as it is today... With the exception of the purely technical recipes... of which many have been found only within the last twenty years... very little has been transferred to our time of this earlier knowledge— which may even have represented a highly developed science of art.
>
> ... although the impressionists destroyed the last remnants of painting theory in their fight against "academicism," they immediately... laid the first foundation stone of a new science of art.
>
> The investigation should proceed in a meticulously exact and precise manner. Step by step, this "tedious" road must be traversed— not the smallest alteration in the nature, in the character, in the effects of the individual elements should escape the watchful eye. Only by means of microscopic analysis can the science of art lead to a comprehensive synthesis, which will extend far beyond the confines of art...[2]

I am impressed by this passage by Kandinsky— by his call for a science of art and by his own method of fulfilling it. Kandinsky made his paintings and wrote about them. He believed that a careful examination of the elements of drawing and painting would lead to a synthesis that would reveal the "truth" of art, of mind, of nature and of spirit; that is, that it would reveal meaning. Today, his work and words (the terminology he used, in particular) remain at issue. The meaning in his words is separated from his paintings. Often it is believed that Kandinsky's "theories" were formulated *before* he made his paintings, and his paintings resulted from his theories. Sometimes a "theory" is understood in such a way that it is said to have nothing to do with his painting. I believe that Kandinsky painted what he saw, noticed what he had painted and wrote about what he noticed.

I am not concerned here with creating, or revealing, a synthesis as Kandinsky directed. I am interested in creating a document that will describe the *event* of my paintings. I want to write about the making and the seeing of my Colour Lock paintings. This is by no means as ambitious a project as Kandinsky had in mind, but for me, it is no less difficult.

To write about painting, a terminology is needed that will separate ideas and distinguish between the events about which one is writing. For painting and for colour there is a lack of terminology. The terminology that is borrowed from other disciplines carries with it the boundaries (and burdens) of those disciplines. However, I believe there is an even greater problem with words; it is in the nature of words.

Consider this: The visual sensation (recept) of a tree stimulates the knowledge (percept) of *that* tree, and permits classification of that tree (concept) with all other trees. This is a pre-verbal event. This event, encompassing recept, percept and concept, does not include the utterance of the word "tree." There need be no knowledge of a word for this event, nor the necessity to form a word, until the observer wishes to communicate the event, or his response to the event, to another person. The observer may speak the word "tree" to another person, and they will agree or disagree on the word and on the event that has been witnessed. Imagine, however, that our observer is alone. He may, on seeing the tree, make an utterance, or he may make a mark (a vertical, perhaps) which signifies his response to the tree. Now, imagine that he makes a second mark, another vertical, which signifies his response to seeing the first mark. The first mark is the signified, and the second mark is the signifier of the first mark. Both marks are the result of an action generated by an idea. Each mark signifies a different idea, and as vertical marks, they are things in themselves.

The observer of the tree has made a drawing; he is an artist. What words will he use to speak about his drawing? What words will he use to speak about the event that incited the first mark, and the event that incited the second mark, and the event he notices in seeing both marks together? The artist has a problem.

Words have always given me a problem. For as long as I've been painting, I have been using words [unsuccessfully] to help direct the viewer toward what is meaningful in my work. Now, I will try write about my paintings. All of the words I will use will be in the service of communicating the event of seeing and the event of making, and the event of seeing what I have made, and to describe the mechanics of what I made and saw in what I made.

The size of the Colour Lock paintings had significance from the start. I wanted the paintings to be an encounter for the viewer on equal physical terms. I am five feet tall; six feet is a common height for an individual. The Colour Lock paintings are about the same size as the viewer. The size I most frequently used is 60" x 60". A 48" x 48" painting is a small work and a large work is 72" x 72". I extended the paintings horizontally to 60" x 120", 72" x 96", 48" x 96" and 48" x 144". Because our eyes are set side by side, our scope of vision is adapted for a wider range horizontally than vertically. The greatest height of any work among the Colour Lock paintings is 77"; the greatest width is 13 feet.

I believe that size is an element in painting. The size and shape of the plane are as important as the size and shape of the elements of the configuration *on* the plane. A large work presents an encounter that requires a viewer to *look it over* by moving his eyes over the surface. The large colour-shapes on the surface direct a viewer's eyes from shape to shape, each shape declaring its colour, filling the eye of the viewer until it moves on to a new colour-shape. Each time the viewer's eye rests it fills with colour; each time the eye moves it seeks equilibrium and finds it in a new colour. Thus, the viewer's eye travels over the entire plane again and again in new sequences; his eye never tires, never loses its equilibrium. The viewer, engaged, may become conscious of this process, may question or account for his response, or he may simply indulge in the satisfaction of the experience— he has begun to see the colour *at work*.

A viewer, however, must take *time* to view the work. A cursory glance will not allow him to experience it. He may, at a glance, believe he has seen it because he is looking to identify the work, to classify it into some predetermined category.

In all of the Colour Lock paintings, I worked to preserve the two-dimensionality of the picture plane. I take seriously Maurice Denis' instruction (1890) to remember that a painting is essentially a flat surface covered with colours arranged in a certain order[3]; it states a fact of the plane that is true for all the paintings in the centuries before Denis and in this century after him. His clear and concise definition of the essential aspects of a painting states not only its planar nature, but it also declares as essential the facts of *colour* and *order*. The planar nature of a painting is confirmed or denied by the elements of colour and order on it.

In the Colour Lock paintings, I preserved the fact of the two-dimensional plane by leaving the canvas surface visible. The canvas is stretched around a stretcher-frame, and no outer frame is added. Three-dimensionality is confined to the "objectness" of the whole structure, and to that object's relationship to the wall on which it hangs.

In my paintings, all of the colour-shapes are positive. I put colour-shape beside colour-shape and so fill up the canvas. Each colour-shape is achieved by a positive action, and each declares itself and its relationships with each other colour-shape. No colour-shape touches the next, so no colour-shape is directly defined by another, but all are interdependent. All of this activity is positive and it is *on* the plane.

The idea that colour advances and recedes is denied by my paintings. Colour can be made to appear to advance and recede, but this illusion can be impeded. By leaving canvas visible around each colour-shape, no colour can recede *into* the plane; the materiality of the canvas does not permit it. No colour advances *from* the plane; the materiality of the colour (pigment rendered opaque) forbids it. Rather, the shape, because of the nature and character of its colour, appears to expand or contract. For instance, yellow is generally believed to advance and can be made to appear to advance readily in certain conditions. In the Colour Lock paintings, a yellow shape can expand into the canvas which surrounds it and the appearance of advancement does not occur. What *is* advancing from the two-dimensional plane to the viewer's eye is the reflected spectral light, as *colour*.

The First Series (1969-1970)

There are 15 paintings in the first series. The title of each work is *Colour Lock Series* and a number, *#1* to *#15*, is added as part of the title. Each painting combines intense colour-shapes and one "grey" shape. The grey shapes are either an intermixture of black and white or, more often, an intermixture of complementary colours and white.

I intermix pigments to make all of my colours. Even the primary colours in my paintings are the result of intermixture. An intense colour is one that declares its hue directly according to what I believe is its nature. A colour to which I have added white pigment must not declare its whiteness over its body colour (that is, become a tint of that colour) but must remain an intensity.

In the first series of paintings the colour interaction is between the *intense* colour-shapes. I believed at the time that the grey of the complementary mixture provided a pause that was colour-active, a pause that modified the contrasts of the intensities and so created a condition of contrast without opposition.

In all of the series of the Colour Lock paintings the character of the *shape* of the colour-shapes is the same. It is a soft-edged shape (as opposed to "hard-edged"). The shapes may best be described as whole, having four loose-edged sides (not straight) and four curved corners (not square). The shapes have the order and energy of geometric shapes, but they are neither geometric shapes nor symbols of geometric shapes. All of the shapes in the Colour Lock paintings are horizontally and vertically disposed. No diagonal occurs.

My method of creating the shapes is simple. I draw with masking tape; that is, I lay tape on the canvas, then tear along its length to form the loose-edge of the shape. When the four sides of the shape have been applied in this way, I complete the corners. I do not seal this masked edge; therefore, when paint is applied within the masked shape the initial applications seep under the edges of the tape. Further applications seal and a surface of colour builds which is dense and opaque. When the tape is removed, the colour-shape has a narrow edge of the paint that bled under the tape during the first applications. On close inspection, this fine margin of thin paint can be seen on each shape. It grips the canvas and reports the substance and materiality of the paint to a viewer.

The Second Series (1970-1972)

There are 18 paintings in the *Colour Lock, Second Series*. The sizes of the works are 60" x 60", 72" x 72", 72" x 96" and 48" x 144". All of the colour-shapes in all of the paintings in the Second Series have the order and energy of the square. All of the shapes in any one painting are the same size. In the square paintings, there are nine shapes— three colours are repeated three times.

The colours are intensities; no greys occur in this series. In the later rectangular paintings, there are 12 shapes— four colours are repeated three times.

Josef Albers has written that any colour can be made to advance or recede. [True.] Victor Vasarely has written that when any one colour is repeated, that colour will appear to recede. [True.] In my paintings, *Colour Lock, Second Series*, all of the colours are repeated and no colour appears to advance or recede.

Albers' examination of the interaction of colour[4] and Vasarely's "colour-form"[5] were particularly important to me when I made this series of paintings. I made and saw each colour; I saw each colour repeated, effecting and effected by itself; I saw each colour effecting and effected by another colour; I saw two colours effecting and effected by a third colour; I saw two colour pairs effecting and effected by each other; I saw all of the colour-shapes at work on the plane.[6]

This body of work confirmed for me the nature of the plane, the nature of illusions and the conditions that affirm or deny them. This work revealed for me an aspect of what I have come to believe is the nature of colour. I saw colours reach for each other and balance each other. The colour activity of these paintings is not into and out of the plane, but up/down, left/right and across, and all of this activity is made visible as colour energy reflected from the surface of the two-dimensional plane to excite the eye and mind.

The Third Series (1972-1974)

There are 12 paintings in the *Colour Lock, Third Series*. In these works, the colours are not regularly repeated, but I did not abandon the repeated colour entirely. In some paintings, I introduced a colour close to black, and in one painting, a coloured grey.

In the Third Series, I used square-like shapes, shapes extended to horizontal rectangles and shapes compressed to vertical rectangles. I believed that when the square-like shape was extended in a direction, or compressed to extend in another direction, the colour of that shape exerted its energy in that direction. The colour-shape, without advancing or receding, acted on the plane with a new emphasis when it had *direction*.

The order that evolved and was sustained in the Second Series was dislocated in the Third Series. I was working with new colours (intensities and blacks and grey), with new shapes (rectangles) on new formats. The sizes of the paintings are 60" x 60", 48" x 64", 48" x 96", 48" x 138" and 60" x 156". In the irregularities of this work I saw another order evolve, and I saw colours behave in new ways.

When I am working toward a painting I draw a pencil sketch, a thumb-nail sketch, of the projected composition. I do not add colour to the sketch because there is no sketching colour medium that has the properties of the opaque intermixtures of the acrylic paint that I use on the painting. Any coloured sketch would be too unlike the colour that will occur on the canvas to be useful. The pencil sketch is a plan for the work. On it, I determine the order and organization of the painting— I consider value relationships; I mark down the names of colours intended for the shapes. I redraw the plan many times, questioning the inherent logic of the projected colour event. I draw arrows to indicate the colour relationships that I believe will come into play. I make notes about those relationships. Always, I am working *toward* the painting, looking for it. I must cover a lot of ground, thinking through that ground that I believe I already know from earlier paintings to find the next step, one that will ask a new question and embody its answer.

The colours named on the sketch can only begin to be realized in the process of mixing pigments. The colour is sought out in intermixture. A colour in the pot is different in appearance from that colour rendered opaque by repeated applications as a large shape on the canvas, and that colour changes again as each new colour is applied to the painting. Each colour goes through changes; each is different wet from dry, large from small, lean from densely applied, and each colour's changes are different from each other colour's changes. All this must be noticed in the process of painting. When I am making a painting, I am not routinely executing my sketches; rather, I am working and watching the painting happen, directing it and being directed by it. The painting is generated by my thoughts and feelings. Those thoughts and feelings are about paint, about colour and shape and their meaning. The painting, completed, is autonomous.

The Black Series (1975-1976)

There are 20 paintings in the *Colour Lock, Black Series*. Those colours that were close to black that I introduced into some of the paintings in the Third Series are the subject of these works. I call them "colour-blacks." I define a colour-black as a colour in its *lowest value ranges*.

Value generally describes the light or dark quality of a colour. Value is represented by a grey scale, that is, a scale that has white at the top, black at the bottom, and regular gradations of grey between the two. The value of a colour is determined theoretically by comparing it to this scale. Each intense colour, that is, each direct hue (red, orange, yellow, green, blue, purple) has a different comparative position in relation to the dark/light scale, and can be described by that relationship. To raise the value of a colour, white is added to it and the result is called a *tint*. To lower the value of a colour, black is added to it and the result is called a *tone*. This is theoretical; it deals with ideal colours to give definition to a particular characteristic of all colour. Pigment, however, is not ideal. It is more complex than the theory implies and its behaviour is determined by its material properties. The stuff of the mind is not the stuff of paint. Theory is supposition, the stuff of the mind; the artist's colours are pigment, the stuff of paint.

To make a colour-black, I do not add black pigment to colours; rather, I add colour (red, yellow, blue) to black pigment to yield a red-black, a yellow-black, a blue-black. The energy of the colour component remains visible; it is not eliminated by the black component, so the colour component of the mixture is active and interacts with other colours and other colour-blacks in the painting. A colour-black, then, is the lowest value of a colour without denying that colour its energy.

In the Black Series, colour-black shapes are combined with intense colour-shapes. In each painting, there are more colour-blacks than intense colours— the balance is toward black. The intense colours are further intensified by contrast. A blue, a green, a purple, each low in value by nature, maintains the balance toward black. A yellow or an orange, each high in value by nature, is modified in intermixture toward black without loss of identity. By modifying the high value colours, I found a broad range of colours that retain their primary or secondary identity and behaviour within the painting. Red, which is considered to be of middle value on the ideal scale, proved to be the most flexible and, therefore the most complex colour. The greatest range of colours are of this hue. An intermixture that was "brown" in the pot, or appeared to be "mud," declared its redness in the painting.

The idea to explore black and to create a balance toward black in these works was in keeping with what I believed is the nature of colour. I have been aware of the peculiar properties of intermixtures of pigments for as long as I have painted, have studied colour and have read colour theory. As interested as I am in analyses of the organization and relationships of colour, I know that no red, no yellow and no blue pigment exists in nature that will behave in the ideal manner basic to theory. Colour theories suppose that there exists a red that reflects only the red light rays, a blue that reflects only the blue light rays and a yellow that reflects only the yellow light rays. In fact, red pigments reflect with the red light rays some of the blue or some of the yellow light rays, or both; blue pigments reflect with the blue light rays some of the red or some of the yellow, or both; yellow pigments reflect with the yellow rays some of the blue or some of the red, or both. "Pure" colour in the theoretically ideal sense does not exist in nature.

Consider red. One red pigment (cadmium) reflects red light rays and some yellow; it can be said to lean toward yellow. Another red pigment (crimson) reflects red light rays and some blue; it can be said to lean toward blue. An intermixture of these two red pigments will yield a new red which is redder, but which is darker— lower in value. The new red combines red, some yellow and some blue. The intermixture of yellow and blue yields green. The new red, then, has a green component. Green is the complement of red and when intermixed with it yields *black*. The new red, while it declares its redness, has begun to move toward black. I believe that all intermixtures of colour (pigments) proceed toward black. This is the nature of colour.

There are vast inconsistencies between theories of colour and the behaviour of coloured matter in the practice of painting.[7] This leads some artists to believe that colour theory is irrelevant to their work. The study of colour is not irrelevant; the theories are merely incomplete. No theory can be used as a formula to be applied to painting, nor can any theory be ignored. On the contrary, a colour-painting (and all painters use colour) reveals the order, the nature and the meaning of colour. But the painter and the viewer must notice it.

In the Black Series the shapes are square-like and there are horizontal and vertical rectangles. Two of the paintings have a vertical format. These two works are the first of my Colour Lock paintings that are taller than wide.

The Grey Series (1976)

There are eight paintings in the *Colour Lock, Grey Series*. Until the Grey Series, all of the colour-shapes in my paintings had been whole shapes; colour filled the shapes unimpeded by eccentricities of shape or direction. In the Grey Series, I introduced a straight-edged shape with square corners. In the earliest paintings in the series (48" x 48"), the straight-edged shape is a horizontal rectangle that occupies an area equal to the two square-like colour shapes in the paintings. In the next painting (66" x 66"), the straight-edged shape is a horizontal rectangle that occupies an area equal to three of the six square-like colour-shapes, and it is at the centre of the composition. In this painting, I consider the rectangle as a square extended both to the left and to the right. The painting that follows is another of the same size in which the straight-edged rectangular shape also extends downward at its centre in place of the square-like shape that occupied that position in the earlier work. In this painting, the straight-edged shape occupies an area equal to four square-like colour-shapes, and I consider it to be a square extended in *three* directions. In the last four paintings in the series (77" x 66"), the loose-edged colour-shapes are rectangles of 1:2 proportion; the straight-edged shape extends in three directions and occupies an area equal to three of the rectangular colour-shapes. These four paintings are taller than wide.

There is one straight-edged shape in each painting in the Grey Series, and it is this shape that, despite its regularity, exhibits the greatest idiosyncrasies of shape. This shape is a “colour-grey.”

I describe a colour-grey as the *tint of a tone* of a colour. I make a colour-grey by adding colour to an intermixture of white and black pigment, to a grey that is more light than dark. The energy of the colour component is diminished, but not negated, by the grey component. In the painting, the colour component is visible and active at the same time as the neutral element of the grey component. A colour-grey (red-grey, yellow-grey, blue-grey) represses the energy of a colour without denying that colour its identity or its activity. In the Grey Series, the intense colour-shapes are made more intense by contrast with the colour-grey shapes. Each intense colour is an intermixture of pigments; each is chromatically dense and direct and it declares its hue as well as that greyed aspect of its nature as it proceeds toward black.

The straight-edged grey shape can be described as a block, a bar and a T-shape of colour. Under all of these conditions, its energy is horizontally or vertically directed, or both. The grey shape is at the centre in each work; it is solid and formal and gives the paintings a bilateral symmetry. The colour of the colour-grey reaches for and interacts with the other colour-shapes which interact with it and with each other. The viewer's eye moves diagonally over the surface of the painting from colour-shape to colour-shape; the eye traces a triangle, an inverted triangle, follows the colours from corner to corner (tracing a square), and it crosses the canvas from corner to opposite corner tracing the diagonals. In these works, the composition is the most static of all of the Colour Lock paintings, yet the paintings exhibit a complex, compounded activity of shape and colour that leads the eye in new directions.

The Vertical Series (1976-1978)

There are 22 paintings in the *Colour Lock, Vertical Series*. In the first eight paintings (66" x 60"), a vertical colour-shape at the centre of the composition extends to the top and bottom edges of the painting. On each side of the vertical shape, a "stack" of square-like and horizontally directed rectangles fill the canvas. Later paintings extend horizontally (66" x 96"); they have two vertical colour-shapes separated by three stacks of colour-shapes— one at the centre and two on each end. In these works, I consider the whole composition to be extended both left and right; they can be viewed as if each vertical shape is the centre of a separate composition in which the middle stack of colour-shapes is common to both. The middle stack of colour-shapes is a vertical of another order and is the true centre of the paintings. The paintings that follow (66" x 84") have three vertical colour-shapes and two stacks of colour-shapes. These paintings have the same composition as the earliest works in this series with the addition of two more vertical colour-shapes at each vertical edge which extend the composition to the left and to the right. The last works in this series (66" x 72") have no vertical shape at the centre of the composition; rather, there are two stacks of colour-shapes side by side at the centre, and two vertical colour-shapes at the left and right edges of the paintings.

There are no colour-blacks or colour-greys in the Vertical Series. There are no eccentric shapes. All of the colour-shapes are whole shapes and whole colours. Each colour-shape is a new colour; that is, no colour is repeated in any work. All of the colours behave as intensities.

The *hue* factor of the colours in this series is extended to its broadest range: red, yellow and blue; orange, green and purple; red-orange, yellow-orange, yellow-green, blue-green, blue-purple and red-purple; red-red-orange, orange-orange-red, orange-orange-yellow, yellow-yellow-orange, yellow-yellow-green, green-green-yellow, green-green-blue, blue-blue-green, blue-blue-purple, purple-purple-blue, purple-purple-red and red-red-purple.

The *value* of the colours is extensive due to the nature of each colour, and this range of values is further extended by the intermixture of pigments. The chromatic factors of any colour established by intermixture undergo changes in the painting as it interacts with each other colour-shape. The earliest paintings in this series bring together seven different colours, then nine different colours. The largest paintings bring together 11 different colours, then 14. There is a lot of colour, and a lot of colour action in these works.

I think it is important that I try to describe the extent of my involvement with colour. In theory, colours are described by particular characteristics: light/dark, warm/cool and (under certain conditions) advancing/receding. Colours are described in terms of their contrasts with each other.[8] Theoretical analyses of colour and the *experience* of colour are of interest to me. I have found no theory unworthy of notice. But colour is a perceptual experience; it is an event, when noticed, that reveals its own order and the order of the mind. Supposition about colour, its nature and its behaviour has been inextricably bound to light. Painters are often believed to be concerned with painting *light and space*. I think it is important to understand that *painters paint paint*, that paint is coloured and it reflects *light* into *space*.

Theories of colour and light ignore or obscure the fact of coloured matter, its complex properties and its behaviour when illuminated by light. Theories that are concerned with light ignore the nature of the "coloured thing" that divides white light like a prism does, reflecting some light rays and absorbing others. Colour theories that deal with the mechanics of the eye examine the physical and chemical character of the eye, and often their goal is to separate individuals into those with normal vision and those with defective vision. Colour theories of the mind examine individuals' responses to colour, isolate the responses common to the greatest number of people, then present those responses as characteristics of the colours. I believe that all of these theories are important, but each is incomplete. Colour theory is fragmented and does not achieve its purpose— to reveal, to inform.

Yet, all these theories are relevant to painting. I suggest that it is *painting* which can unite the diversity of theories. The will of the painter, the act of painting, the manifestation of that act of will in the object created, all this is preserved and made visible. Every work of art throughout history reveals and informs. Every painting throughout history is coloured, is made with pigment. That pigment is isolated into "pure" hue, intermixed to yield new hues, modified to yield new energy, or to be de-energized, apportioned in greater and lesser areas, constricted to "lines" and extended to shapes— all this occurs in all paintings. To ignore colour in art is to ignore it in life. We live in a coloured world, and that fact has been true since the world began, since matter first formed and light first fell upon it.

In the Vertical Series, shape is given greater direction than in previous series and the colour activity is greater. The verticals are the most active colour-shapes in terms of direction, but the extension of a vertical to the extremities of the canvas puts its one colour in *constant* relationship with each colour-shape in the stacks. The stacked colour-shapes are less active in terms of their direction, but their size, position and colours put them in *constantly changing* relationship with the vertical colour-shape and with each other. The vertical colour-shapes separate and embrace the stacks of colour-shapes. The colour interaction in these works leads the eye in oblique and diagonal directions across a composition where the shapes are only horizontally and vertically disposed. It is because of colour interaction that the viewer's eye moves and rests and moves again, stimulated by colour, colour pairs and colour contrasts in constantly changing interrelationships and their constant interdependence. It is coloured light rays that reach the viewer's eye reflected from the coloured pigment on the plane. It is in the *space* between the viewer and the colours viewed, and in the *time* of that space, that the *event* of colour occurs and yields up its meaning.

The Black and Grey Series (1978-1980)

Words are common coin— everyone has them; everyone uses them; everyone passes them out freely and in exchange for others' words. Words have meaning. One word can have several meanings. Some words have so many meanings that they are difficult to use and are not helpful. Words that are simple and clear serve best to describe painting, but one must use a lot of them. Words follow one another in speech and in writing, and it is along a careful path of words that ideas are communicated. The ideas that are communicated by words about a painting are not the event of the painting— idea is *conceptual*; a painting is a *perceptual* event. However, I believe that words and ideas can open the avenues of the mind to a new receptivity, to a greater consciousness so that perception can occur and the importance of perception can be grasped.

There are 16 paintings in the *Colour Lock, Black and Grey Series*. To some extent, this series is a summing up of the series that pre-date it. Like the Second Series and the Grey Series, it is orderly and often symmetrical. Like the Vertical Series, some shapes are strongly directed and the larger works are extended compositions of the smaller works. Like the Black Series, it has colour-blacks; like the Grey Series, it has colour-greys; like both of these series, it combines colour-blacks and colour-greys with intense colours. If there is a summing up in this series, it, too, extends and reveals for me the order and energy of colour.

The following dated passages are excerpts from my personal journals.

7 October, 1978.

I'm into a big think. I have taken a new direction in my sketches and I'm making progress. I'm working with a horizontal/vertical composition... a square format. The configuration is a "cross" completed by four shapes...

17 November, 1978.

I have a piece of canvas stretched and prepared [for *Colour Lock, Black and Grey Series #1*]. I spent today mixing colours. I will use blacks, greys and intensities. Today's mixing didn't give me the "right" colours. I will mix again tomorrow. All is suspended...

26 December, 1978.

I am into new work and it is going well now. First painting [66" x 72"] was very difficult; the second, exciting— an affirmation of the first and I believed I was into something. I have completed the third and am presently working toward the fourth...

17 January, 1979.

This work opens up new colour relationships. The blacks and greys in each painting are the lowest and highest value colours. The intense colours fall inside the range of these values. There is another aspect, difficult to define, that has to do with a contrast of *character* that separates any black or grey from any intense colour, and any grey from either the blacks or the intense colours. The greys are most flexible. They relate to both the high value intense colours and to the low value blacks. One might expect that these paintings with both blacks and greys would not be colourful, but that's not true; they are surprisingly colourful...

Albers says that the values of two colours [which are close in value] compared with the naked eye can't be correctly discerned beyond guess-work, i.e. it is almost impossible to determine which of the two colours is the higher or lower in value. He has found a way to determine comparative value which involves overlapping [swatches of] the two colours and allowing a successive reaction of the eye to occur.[9] I question what is happening with this method... The important fact is that the eye cannot accurately discern the relative values of the two colours.

Somehow this is relevant to the paintings I am making and it has to do with the behaviour of the greys. A colour-grey has a black component that relates to the colour-blacks, a colour component that relates to the intense colours, and a value factor that relates to each other colour/value factor in the painting. There are so many contrasts occurring between the colour-greys and every other colour in the painting, that it may be this highly flexible characteristic of the greys that makes them neutral. I use the word "neutral" meaning something that takes *all* sides, rather than takes *no* side.

5 May, 1979.

I completed my painting today [*Colour Lock, Black and Grey Series #9*]. I made some changes as I was mixing colour. These are not opposing hue changes like changing red to blue, but rather, a green was changed to a blue-blue-green, another to a green-green-blue. These two colours suppress their yellow... This is something I must write down. Somehow I must describe the nuance of every colour in words...

1 May, 1980.

I have a new painting [*Colour Lock, Black and Grey Series #14*]. This one [66" x 114"] came together more easily than the last. It has an overall red/blue contrast... reds collect on the left, blues collect on the right, and each relates to and encompasses a yellow at the centre. Unusual balance. This piece has more colour-blacks than colour-greys. The reverse is true in the last painting...

4 July, 1980.

I sized my canvas today[10] with the intention of beginning [*Colour Lock, Black and Grey Series #16*]... weather is hot... will put off beginning... my head is ready, except for the blacks— I keep moving them [in my sketch]— so I guess I'm not really ready yet.

I want this painting to have low colours. A red will be the highest value colour. I want two colour-greys and four colour-blacks and two different blues, two different greens, two different purples and two different reds. These last paintings (and this final one) are about red/blue contrast.

In #15, there are four colour-greys and three colour-blacks. The four greys interrupt the order of the intense colour-shapes: red, blue and orange. It is a formal composition and the greys "walk" through it in a staggered manner calling attention to themselves, their colour, their lack of order, in contrast to the order and balance of the intense colour-shapes and the composition as a whole. I hope I will be as successful with this final work...

The Eighth Series (1980-1982)

25 September, 1980.
I have been working toward new paintings. I consider working with colour-shapes on a coloured field or ground. All of the Colour Lock paintings have had a natural canvas ground... I have decided to continue with the horizontal/vertical...

To paint the field or ground sounds like a small change to make, but it will affect everything. I consider working with thin transparent applications of colour to retain the texture of the canvas. I want to avoid "object to ground" and that near/far activity that can occur when contrasting colours abut. I want a side to side, up, down and across activity of colour reaching for colour. I will have to think through a painting in terms of *colour pairs* since each colour-shape will be acting with the ground colour (as well as with every other colour-shape). By moments, I think the problems are insurmountable.

So far, I can only sketch and draw and think and think colour. I think about blacks, about colour-blacks on a "black" ground, about colour-greys on a black ground and intense colour-shapes acting with colour-blacks and greys, and even tints and white on a coloured ground. The ground colour will add a new contrast. Any ground colour I choose will be lower in value than the natural coloured ground I have been working on. The colour-shapes will rise and lower in value in their relationship to the coloured ground... I have a lot to think about.

15 October, 1980.

Completed my painting [*Colour Lock, Eighth Series #2*]. This painting [48" x 48"] has a [thinly applied] blue-black ground. There are three colour-shapes— a horizontal red shape is at the top, a vertical orange shape is at the left and a blue-grey shape, almost square, is at the right. The red and orange are brilliant, but they have been slightly lowered [in intermixture]. The blue-grey appears to be almost white. This is because of its contrast with the intensities and the ground colour.

I have lost all of my certainty about my colour. I test each colour on a piece of natural canvas and on a piece of coloured canvas that I prepare at the same time as the ground of the painting. I know most about the colour on the natural canvas, but the same colour on the piece of coloured canvas is entirely different, a new experience, and that colour applied to the large canvas changes again. So I am uncertain. I proceed when it seems right... There is a lot to find out.

The colour-greys are a big surprise. I expected that they would rise in value on a coloured ground, but their approach to white is more than I anticipated. The colour components in the greys and blacks are more active here. A colour is as active here when it is indirect as when it is direct...

24 October, 1980.

I completed my painting [*Colour Lock, Eighth Series #3*]. There are four colour-shapes— blue, green, yellow and red-grey— on a red-black ground. The blue shape, a vertical on the left, is the largest because it is the full height of the painting, Beside it at the top is a horizontal yellow shape, and a vertical green shape is at the centre. The vertical red-grey shape is at the right.

This is a red/yellow/blue painting, too. Blue and yellow are directly present and they are combined in the green shape. Red is indirect, visible in the red-grey shape and in the red-black of the ground colour. This red, a crimson, leans toward blue, so there is a suggestion of purple. The intermixture for the blue shape is strong with ultramarine which leans toward red, so it also has a suggestion of purple. The yellow is quite brilliant— a difficult colour. I believe I have been successful with it here.

The highest contrast is between the blue and green pair and the yellow and red-grey pair. The strongest "lock" occurs because of that contrast. That is not a contradiction.

There are direct relationships here: the blue shape and the yellow shape (primary contrast), the green shape and the indirect reds (complementary contrast), the blue, yellow and green shapes (primary/secondary contrast)... The red-grey approaches white and pairs with the yellow shape— both are high in value. The ground colour fluctuates as it effects and is effected by each colour-shape. The value of the [transparent] ground colour contrasts with the dark colours and, although distinctly different from the high value colours, melds with them and sometimes seems to be of like value. I think I have hold of something worth pursuing...

9 November, 1980.

I want to write something about my one-colour-theory. This will be difficult because it can all be said in two sentences. It is a perceptual theory, so I begin there: to see colour requires 1) a coloured thing, 2) light and 3) the eye. It is in this framework that my one-colour-theory works.

The one colour is red. When red is seen, green appears (by simultaneous or successive reaction of the eye). Green is blue and yellow. So, by seeing one colour, red, the primary colours are revealed. All colours are intermixtures of these three colours: red, yellow and blue.

Question: why choose red? Each of the primary colours will call up its complement by simultaneous or successive reaction, so why not choose yellow or blue? My reason: red is most visible. Because of its position in the spectrum, we see red first. And the values of red and green are more like than those of blue and orange or yellow and purple. The likeness in value of the red/green pair makes it more accessible to the eye. My one-colour-theory is about perception— the more natural the event, the more true. Each of the other two primaries will work and can be made to work logically, but red works most naturally.

4 December, 1980.

I have put a lot of headwork into this painting, but even now I'm not sure. The energy and activity of primary colour contrasts is difficult to sustain. Somehow, restraint is necessary, particularly with yellow which doesn't have the *weight* of the other two colours. I think about Mondrian and I am awed by the fact that he controlled these highly energized colours so well, and so often...

6 December, 1980.

I completed [*Colour Lock, Eighth Series #5*]... The red, yellow and blue shapes read as primaries. However, the blue has been moved toward green so it will link with the red. The red has been lowered and moved slightly toward blue. The red remains brilliant, intensified by the yellow which has been lowered, too, and moved toward red, then opened slightly with white so it will work with the grey.

The grey is a red-grey, but this combination of red (crimson) and black in the grey yields a purple-grey. The yellow shape is close in value to the grey and also relates to it by complementary contrast. The red shape reaches for the red in the grey; the blue shape reaches for its blue.

The black shape is a yellow-black and it can be read as both yellow-black and green-black. Its yellow factor is balanced by the intense yellow shape at the other side of the canvas. The greenness of the black shape plays with the blue shape which has been moved toward green, so as a green-black, it draws off the greenness of the blue leaving the blue shape intensely blue in its place.

The black shape and the blue shape are closest in value. The red/blue contrast is at the centre of the painting. The red shape and the yellow shape, both high value and intense, can be separated from the "dark" side of the painting.

The black shape and the grey shape link as "neutral" colours, a contrast to the intensities and they are opposite in value.

The black, grey and yellow shapes "frame" the red and blue shapes.

The blue, red and yellow shapes link as primary colours to form a square at the right which is framed on two sides by the black and the grey shapes.

Alternately, the black, blue and red shapes link as a "dark" square at the left which is framed by the yellow and grey shapes, both like in value.

There are five colour-shapes in this painting. Four are equal in size, shape and direction. The fifth shape extends in size and has a different direction— it is a horizontal shape. The four vertical shapes are in direct opposition to it, and so is the viewer.

The eye can begin anywhere. Start with red, the most immediate and accessible colour. The red shape and the red-grey shape are like in hue, but they also contrast— contrast of direction, horizontal and vertical. Because of the purple character of the red-grey shape, the eye moves easily to the blue shape to pair the blue and grey shapes. The yellow and yellow-black shapes will each pair with the grey shape as complements and they can frame the rest of the painting in each case and when all three are taken together. Or, the red and blue shapes and the horizontal grey shape can gather as a T-shape bound by the yellow and yellow-black shapes. This can go on and on; the painting works.

The ground colour is a blue-black; it reads as a blue-grey and is about middle value. The highest value colour-shapes are lighter than the ground colour; the lowest are darker. The thin transparent application of the ground colour leaves the texture of the canvas visible. The colour-shapes act on it. They neither advance nor recede from it or from each other. The two-dimensionality of the plane is intact...

16 February, 1981.

I think about Vincent van Gogh's comment about black and white being the fourth complementary pair.[11] I like this idea. Black and white are not regarded as colours because they are not spectral hues. However, all colours (pigments) when intermixed proceed toward black. Each secondary colour yielded from the (subtractive) intermixture of two primary colours is greyed or on its way toward black. A case could be made for the primaries: yellow approaches white (yellow is the lightest hue) and blue approaches black (blue is the darkest primary hue).

Black is the intermixture of all colours, or more simply, the intermixture of red, yellow and blue. White, because it is a pigment, could be described as one that lacks hue— white is the absence of hue. It is the converse with light (additive colour); white is yielded when all the spectral hues are gathered, and black is the absence of light.

In theory, when complementary pairs are intermixed they yield a neutral grey. This is only true in practice if white is added to the mixture. But it is true of white and black in both theory and in practice. No problem there.

On the colour wheel, complementary colours are directly opposite each other. Since there is no place for black and white on the wheel, I can't describe them this way. However, black could be placed inside at the centre of the wheel, and white placed outside the wheel. White could be a "finite" [or "infinite"] hue for each colour on the wheel.

The position of the complementary pairs on the wheel describes their relationship. Each is directly opposite (it completes and opposes the other) in *hue*. White and black are directly opposite in *value*. There are complementary pairs that are neither primary nor secondary colours: red-purple/yellow-green or red-orange/blue-green. But Vincent said that black and white were the *fourth* pair, so he must be adding them to the primary and secondary colours. Could it follow that one of them is a primary and the other is a secondary?

The three complementary pairs are red/green, blue/orange and yellow/purple. If I choose yellow, red and blue, the primaries in this order show a progressively lowering value. So do orange, green and purple; but the order that is parallel to that order of the primaries is purple, green and orange, and that shows the secondaries in a progressively rising value. So?

The pairs differ in value contrast when one pair is compared to the next. The yellow/purple pair has the greatest contrast, the blue/orange has less and red/green has the least. Considering the white/black pair in this framework, its value contrast is greater than the yellow/purple pair. White is higher in value than yellow; black is lower in value than purple. In terms of parallel values, could white be considered a primary and black, a secondary?

I wonder about Mondrian and his use of the three primary colours and white, black and grey. Would Mondrian consider both white and black to be primaries? In terms of the primary colours, white is higher than yellow and black is lower than blue. Intermixed, black and white yield grey— as a secondary? This is consistent with the intermixture of two primaries— they yield a secondary. But black and white can't be mixed with any other primary to yield a new secondary hue; rather, they yield another colour of the same hue that is changed in value and chroma. So much for that.

As a fourth complementary pair, with only white considered a primary, white can't be mixed with other primaries to yield a secondary hue. The fourth pair won't intermix like other hues. White and black have some characteristics that are consistent with the hue pairs, but they will not intermix with them to yield new hues or new pairs. So, they are a unique pair. White and black affect the value of any colour with which they are intermixed without changing the hue of that colour.

This is not fair to Vincent. He called black and white the fourth complementary pair, and he used them directly as colours.

4 July, 1981.

I have the new painting [*Colour Lock, Eighth Series #14*] leaning against the easel-boards with #12 and #13 on each side of it. When I see all three paintings [each 72" x 72"], I am happy with the red, blue and yellow shapes (the largest shape in each painting) on their purple, green and orange ground colours.

In #14, the orange ground and the yellow shape on it, both intense and high-keyed, seemed risky to try make work. The absence of either a colour-black or a colour-grey in this painting also seemed daring. My intention seemed like a contradiction: to use no neutral colours, but to bring about another kind of neutrality by using intermediate colours. The idea that intermediate colours by the nature of their intermixtures would supply a greyness is logical, and it appears to be true. But even now, I don't know the more or less of it... The greyness that I was after is subtle. No colour appears to be directly greyed in the completed work, but I believe that it is the greyness of each intermixture that is controlling the activity of the painting. The colours do not rush at the eye. There is a sense of stillness in this highly coloured work...

I see faults in my language. The words red, yellow and blue don't describe my intermixtures of these colours. Often, I will describe a colour as a secondary when it is closer to an intermediate colour. As well, I have no way to describe the greyed aspect of an intermixed colour. The relationships I try to describe are more complex than my words imply. I prefer to call colours by their "family" names. I believe that *everything depends on red, yellow and blue*. The theoretical red, yellow and blue don't exist. The *particular* red, yellow and blue that I write about are not described by the language I am using. The ground colours are also a problem. They are transparent; the colour names don't describe that or their activity.

7 June, 1982.

... I have been thinking about something I have to call "colour function." I have been trying to describe the activity of colours. By describing colours and their components in terms of contrasts, I don't learn anything new, but I think I am extending my understanding of those things I have known. Earlier I described a colour that *leaned*, or that I had *bent*, toward another colour as a primary or secondary colour. Now I am more aware of the nuance of activity that bending a colour brings about. All this seems to me to be part of the order and nature of colour.

To articulate this visually is difficult; to articulate it verbally seems impossible. However sophisticated or unsophisticated one's understanding of colour is, *it will function*, but words almost deny that function. My new understanding seems so large in my head and has such far-reaching ramifications— I am disappointed by my failure to write it down.

9 June, 1982.

... in the new painting [*Colour Lock, Eighth Series #16*], the red ground is pretty active. It is changed in appearance by the colour-shapes on it from red to red-orange and even to orange. It acts with each colour-shape making some aspect of each colour-shape more or less active. For instance, the blue-green shape which in intermixture was made more blue than green declares its greenness because of the red ground colour. Although I have bent the secondary (green) to an intermediate colour (blue-green), the red ground colour insists on its greenness and *bends it back again.* With the red-orange shape, the red ground claims the red of the shape bending the colour back to orange. One can see the intermediate nature of each colour, but an equilibrium is brought about by this activity. The ground colour is functioning in a different way with each colour-shape, and in some relationships it will sacrifice its own identity as red.

The red of the ground is an intermixture of two cadmiums and a small amount of crimson. The cadmiums lean toward yellow; the crimson, toward blue. The combination will be greyed. However, with this red the eye doesn't register the greyness, but it is there in the inherent complementary factor, and because of it, I achieve a balanced colour for the eye. The eye requires equilibrium. If I supply that equilibrium, the eye will become neither fatigued nor confused as it moves over the painting. This is the consequence of intermixture. Sometimes I exploit it; I make a distinctly greyed colour function as a primary or secondary colour.

There is something else that can be finely tuned— I'll call it "colour-value." It is different than dark/light value. I don't know how to name what I'm doing.

21 July, 1982.

... I have been thinking about my habit of lowering colours. When pigments are intermixed, they yield a greyed colour; this is only part of my inclination to lower colours. There is something else. Consider a scale of colour-value that has yellow at the top and purple at the bottom. Yellow is primary; purple is binary. The primaries, then, are yellow (high), red (middle) and blue (low). The binary colours, orange and green, are within the frame of the primaries on the scale. There are no colours above yellow, but purple is below blue. Purple is an odd-man and creates a problem. The most common solution to the problem is to tint purple, to raise its value by adding white to make a "mauve" or "violet" that is parallel in value to any one of the other colours. I see this done in paintings most often. I don't do it; rather, I preserve the intense low character of purple and I lower the other colours.

This may explain my difficulty with yellow— I lower yellow the most, most often, and always question why I am doing it. Do I compromise yellow when I lower it? I think not because the painting works with the lowered yellow. In the completed painting, all the colours raise in colour-value and behave as intensities.

Seen in this light (if this idea has any merit) my use of colour-blacks (colour in its lowest value ranges) was a logical step for me to take; that I avoid tints of colours (I consider a tint to be a de-energized colour) can be explained; it supports the colour-greys (the tint of a *tone* of a colour). My intention to use white as a colour will raise a bigger problem than I thought.

Yellow may be a difficult colour because of purple— purple rather than yellow is the culprit. I will have to think about this...

15 August, 1982.

I have finished my painting [*Colour Lock, Eighth Series #19*]. The ground colour is red. Crimson dominates the intermixture and it has been modified by burnt sienna, burnt umber (both "reds") and small amounts of yellow and blue. What was dark red-brown in the pot becomes a rich low red on the painting [72" x 96"].

The longest shape is the red horizontal at the top. The yellow and orange shapes stand vertically at the left and right. These three colour-shapes "frame" the yellow-black shape and the large blue shape at the centre. The painting works smoothly.

The blue and yellow-black shapes pair easily because of their like value. The "frame" of red, yellow and orange shapes contrasts with the centre pair. The blue and orange shapes which are side by side are complements. The yellow and yellow-black shapes pair by their like hue and contrast in value. The red ground and the red shape have a specific relationship to each of the other four colour-shapes.

Red, yellow and blue are whole and direct in this painting. A red/green contrast occurs indirectly: the red shape relates to the "greenness" of the yellow-black shape. A yellow/purple contrast occurs even more indirectly: the yellow shape relates to the "purpleness" of the ground colour. This "settles" the yellow.

In this painting (and in the last one), I have put yellow in its highest contrast to all the other colours and it does not leave the painting. Since I questioned my reasons for lowering yellow, I am working differently with it. I lower it less now because I think I understand better the range of its activity. Here, a yellow shape is beside a yellow-black shape and below a red shape. It is in greatest opposition to its surrounding colours— it has the greatest value contrast to the yellow-black and is in direct hue contrast to the red. The indirect "purpleness" of the ground colour completes the yellow leaving the yellow shape and the yellow-black shape free to behave in greatest opposition to each other.

My earlier decisions to lower yellow were less informed. Now, I lower yellow to a particular place for a particular reason. I think my painting works, and it has particular importance to me because of the yellow.

15 September, 1982.
This last painting [*Colour Lock, Eighth Series #20*] speaks well for the whole series. The large yellow-grey shape reaches back to some of the earliest paintings in the series. The primary and complementary concerns here have evolved out of this series. It is the yellow ground colour that takes this last painting one step further, and takes every aspect of the painting further with it. I believe I am moving toward *white* as a colour-shape. This painting with its yellow ground and large yellow-grey shape moves in that direction, but is just shy of it.

Now that I am more aware of yellow, I don't know how I will "manage" white. The tendency for intermixtures to become greyed, and the significance of that fact in intermixtures of yellow make me question my concept of white. Pissarro says that grey is part of the colours in nature. I say that grey is part of the nature of colours. But what is white?

It may be that white pigment, as it comes from the tube, will be as useless to me as black from the tube. When I use "black" it is as *colour* in its lowest value ranges. I use "grey" as the tint of a tone of *colour*. Perhaps the "white" I propose to use will have to be *colour in its highest value ranges*. Will that mean a tint? I have avoided tints for years; they are de-energized colour.

If "white" had a hue factor, it would function as that hue functions. Just as pure black does not exist, so pure white may not exist. A white with colour added could behave as a colour and still declare its whiteness, and it would be perceived as "white." Maybe this is where I'm going.

These excerpts from my journals describe some of my concerns over the period I made the 20 *Colour Lock, Eighth Series* paintings. The emphasis is on colour, its interrelatedness, its function, and the experience of a specific "colour-value."

My journals give me a means of sorting ideas about my paintings by translating what I see and what I believe I know about what I see into words. It is through this translation that the "self-conscious rightness" of my painting is tested. By "self-conscious rightness," I mean "intuition." The test of words examines the thoughtful element that resides in intuition.

In the process of making a painting, I do *what seems most right*. That rightness is informed by both a self-consciousness (intuition) and a consciousness that I will call "intelligence." Intuition and intelligence are informed by the phenomena in the world of nature. A painter is informed in this way, but he also makes phenomena occur each time he makes a painting. His "world" is his painting; his "science" is the examination of the phenomena of his world.

It is fair for any artist to ask of himself: What am I doing and why am I doing it?— and, What have I done, how does it work and what does it mean? It was while making the Eighth Series that I began to test my consciousness most thoroughly by translating into words as much as I could about my questions and answers. I drew on ideas I had learned elsewhere, tested those ideas against what I saw in my work and began to formulate new ideas when conventional ideas failed. Sometimes I modified a conventional idea; sometimes I had to abandon it and adapt a more radical idea. I questioned those radical ideas that have been expressed in other painters' writings. My own experience gave me confidence in the authority of the paintings and the writings of artists.

When an artist writes about his work, he has to use words. However, even while using them, the artist *denies the authority of words*. His writing is in the service of his painting, the visually perceived event. If this is understood, the reader can *enter into the idea*. If the reader can't do this, he will examine the words as authority, classify them, find contradictions and discredit the artist's idea.

The artist who writes is faced with a dilemma of percept/concept duality. The artist communicates in his paintings— they are full of meaning and are his first and fullest statement. They are visual event, and the viewer must see them as perceptual, as they are made. The artist's writings communicate his concepts about the perceptual event, but do not replace it. Concept follows percept laterally, not vertically. It is the peak of the vertically directed *percept* that the artist writes about (about, as if around). The concepts he deals with in his speech and in his writing serve to clarify that peak of perception. Unfortunately, the artist's concepts are often misinterpreted; they are believed to present the ideas *represented* in the paintings. Complex extrapolations are built upon the artist's words extending them laterally in every direction. The painting, then, is viewed as symbolic.

In writing this document of my work, I am avoiding analogy as much as I can. My journals are laborious descriptions of the idea and the event of the perceived painting and the mechanics of achieving it materially. This is deliberate; I want to prevent any extrapolation away from the point of the painting or the peak of perception. If anywhere in this essay a reader has found something he thinks *may* be true, but which he has not *noticed* before, then I have accomplished something here. If, while reading the details in the journal excerpts, a reader felt frustrated by the complexities and found himself thinking: You *really* have to *see* the painting— then I have achieved by my writing precisely what any painter wants to achieve with words. The reader cannot see my paintings here. Even if this book should contain the finest colour reproductions of my paintings, that substitute would not compensate.

My one-colour-theory (9 November, 1980) is a fragile deduction, but it is eminently useful to me. As "theory," it bridges pigment, coloured light and the eye and mind. Although fragile, it is a synthesis. In my journals, I have often written: All is red, yellow and blue. It is from painting, making and seeing my paintings that I have come to recognize the measure and meaning of that idea.

My examination of Vincent's "fourth complementary pair" (16 February, 1981) is playful, but it is this kind of play that shows the arbitrary nature of conventional ideas. Colour theories are conventions; that is, each theory is structured conveniently to satisfy an hypothesis. The three predominant areas of colour theories— coloured matter, coloured light rays, physical and psychological colour response— use conventions that are separate and divided from each other. Each area has a different structure; each supports its own hypothesis and neglects the other two. There is no credible synthesis that supports all three outside of painting. A painting is the will of the artist, the substance of pigment, the phenomenon of coloured light rays, the process of seeing and knowing, and the order of all of these. It is the viewer's will for art that brings him to the painting. It is among painters that "theorists" can be found who try to address all of this. But painting is not theory; it is *event*. To describe that event in words invariably creates contradictions.

My idea of "colour function" (7 June, 1982) shows my own contradictions in writing. I thought I should and could write down everything I see in my work and everything I know about what I see. The means of doing it is words and the context out of which I must take those words is the language of theory. Over and over again, the event of the painting denies the theory. The event declares its own meaning; the theory must be restructured. But I am not satisfied to dispense with theory, or to forego the transcription of a painting's meaning into words; rather, I believe that words have an essential role to play. Words can state what has been noticed, they can direct the eye and mind to notice, and *noticing* is perception.

My term "colour-value" (9 June, 1982) is not defined in the journal entries here. The term names my suspicion that "value" as an isolated characteristic of colour is a mere convenience of theory. Dark/light value (the grey scale) in theory is parallel to the hue scale. But "dark" and "light" do not exist independent of hue. That which is "dark" is not simply that which reflects less light, but that which reflects a particular amount and a particular number of spectral (coloured) light rays. That which is "light" must be described in the same way. The idea that dark/light value is other than coloured cannot be upheld. Black and white are colours. When the eye sees black and knows it is seeing black, it is because it is receiving coloured light rays. When the eye sees white and knows it is seeing white, it is because it is receiving coloured light rays. The experience of black and white is the same as the experience of colour.

These ideas— the one-colour-theory, Vincent's fourth complementary pair, colour function and colour-value— are interdependent. Their significance led me to "white."

The White Series (1983)

There are 10 paintings in the *Colour Lock, White Series*. In nine of the paintings, one white shape is combined with intense colour-shapes on a coloured ground; the last painting has two white shapes. The "white" is a colour-white; that is, it is white pigment with colour added. A colour-white has an active hue factor and it declares its whiteness. A colour-white is colour in its highest value ranges. My "colour-value," as opposed to dark/light value, is made manifest in this series of paintings.

There are no colour-black or colour-grey shapes in these paintings. The intense colour-shapes are primary and secondary in character. The darkest colours, blue, purple and green, function as intense colours as well as like "black." The intermixed colours which become greyed function as intense colours and like "grey." All the colour-shapes, however, remain bright and clear, dense and intense by interaction and interdependence.

My "colour-function" is visible in this series. I had seen that a colour which was not a primary colour could be made to behave like a primary in a painting where no true primary was present. An intermixture that had been moved to an intermediate colour could return to a primary by interaction. The paintings in this series report redness, yellowness and blueness as if directly through indirect colours.

The use of colour-white in this series clarified for me something of the meaning of "white" and the meaning of *light*.

The organization of the shapes in the paintings, like earlier works, is horizontal/vertical. The event of colour moves the eye up, down, side to side and diagonally over the paintings.

From September of 1982 to March of 1983, I asked myself: What is white? I completed the first painting of the White Series on the 23rd of March, and I continued to ask my question. I tried to write down everything I noticed in each painting (not religiously— this exercise is tiresome even for me). It was my consciousness of the complexity of the event of colour and the movement of the eye as it receives that event that led me to *time* as a visual element. I was confronted with the idea of a time-space, and what has been called "the fourth dimension" in art.

Time, understood as "duration" is relevant to painting. A painting is made during a period of time and a viewer must take time to view it. Time, understood as "moment," is relevant to painting, in the making and the seeing and the knowing. Time-space, which I understood as the time and space that all objects occupy, and through which all light passes, is a concept that satisfies my idea of painting as event in its largest and most profound sense. The painting (the three-dimensional object) occupies time and space. The surface of the painting (the two-dimensional plane) on which colours are assembled in a particular order, reflects light into space in all directions all of the time. All objects in nature occupy space, are seen as surfaces, and reflect light. The painting is a new object in nature created by an artist. It has a particular surface which reflects particular light rays to a viewer's eye and into time and space. The colour that reflects more light rays than any other colour is white. White pigment reflects more light in all directions, all of the time.

I thought about Malevich, about his white, his "eternal white," his white of infinite space. I knew there were many views among artists and in science about time-space [space-time] and the idea of "the fourth dimension." I was both curious and resistant to the idea of time-space. I began to read sources, and I painted the White Series.

By September, I knew without doubt that when I had done all I could do in this series of paintings, all of the Colour Lock series, the work of 15 years, would be finished. At first I was shocked by this realization, then fearful and reluctant to address it. When I did, I was liberated by it. I began to wonder about the next step, about what could open up for me. But the work at hand was the White Series; I could go nowhere until I saw this work completed.

16 October, 1983.
I work further on my sketches for my next painting [*Colour Lock, White Series #10*]. I have made a change that may or may not affect the work as I conceived it. It is not a change in the direction of the work, but a change that recognizes the character of yellow.

I have found yellow such a difficult colour. This work with white expands the framework in which yellow acts. What I have regarded as the inflexibility of yellow has made me shy of the colour. Only yesterday while I was thinking through the sketches again did I see the flexibility of yellow. It is so simple.

I have had problems because of the apparent lack of density of yellow. Sometimes I resolve this by mixing the cadmium yellows with yellow oxide [ochre]. I've pressed yellow toward orange and toward yellow-green, but in each case I believed I was moving yellow away from its own character. Yesterday, I realized that that orangeness and that greenness *are* the character of yellow.

In #8, I worked with a red (toward blue) and a red (toward yellow). In #9, I worked with a blue (toward red) and a blue (toward yellow). Now I understand that yellow has particular characteristics, too; it has this same flexibility. I recognize a yellow (toward red) and a yellow (toward blue). I'm not sure how this will affect the painting. I may know more about yellow, but I will have to see if I will make more by it.

I completed the last painting in the White Series on 22 October, 1983. In December, I began to make new paintings.

November, 1984.
Toronto

Notes:

1. See: J.C. Le Blon. *Coloritto* (ca. 1720). (Facsimile edition: Van Nostrand, Reinhold, 1980)

2. Wassily Kandinsky. *Point and Line to Plane*. (Dover, N.Y., 1979)

3. Maurice Denis' essay "Definition du neo-traditionnism," written under the pen-name Pierre-Louis, was published in 1890 in the review, *Art et Critique*. In the first paragraph: "Remember that before it is a war-horse, a naked woman or a trumpery anecdote, a painting

is essentially a flat surface covered with colours assembled in a certain order." The essay was included in Denis' collected writings, *Theories*, published in 1912. Cit. pp. 149-150. Wladyslawa Jaworska. *Gauguin and the Pont-Avon School*. (New York Graphic Society, 1972)

4. Josef Albers. *Interaction of Colour*. (Yale University Press, 1971)

5. Victor Vasarely. *Vasarely* and *Vasarely II*. (Griffon Neuchatel, 1969 and 1970)

6. I am using the verb "effect" meaning "to bring about" to emphasize that colours are *brought into being* and a painting is *brought into being* by the interaction of colour.

7. Scientific theories of colour are generally concerned with light and vision. Questions about the properties of pigments have been the province of painters and chemists.

8. Johannes Itten. *The Art of Colour*. (Van Nostrand, Reinhold, 1973)

9. Op. cit. pp. 12-15.

10. The verb "to size," used here, describes the application of a glue-size to a canvas support. The traditional technique is to apply the glue before applying gesso or white ground to prepare the canvas to receive paint. The "size" I am referring to is acrylic emulsion. The natural canvas surface of my paintings is prepared with two applications of reduced emulsion to create a surface that will receive the paint and will give some protection to those areas of canvas that remain visible.

11. *The Complete Letters of Vincent van Gogh*. 3 vol. (New York Graphic Society, Second Edition, 1981) See Vol. III. B22, p. 527.

Small Paintings.

Size is an element in painting. Until 1984, my paintings were large; these new works are small. In them, I explore the dimension of smallness, that particular of size, and I explore the painting as object and as surface. The surface is paint; the paint is colour. Colour, its interaction and its interdependence, is the subject and the meaning of these works.

Red, yellow, blue, black, white and grey, I will call a primary and primal colour-grammar. Red, red toward blue and red toward yellow; yellow, yellow toward red and yellow toward blue; blue, blue toward yellow and blue toward red— a vocabulary of colour nuance. "Black" is primal, always made of red, yellow and blue. White is always a colour-white which contrasts by its whiteness and interacts by its hue. Grey is primal black and white together. All is red, yellow and blue.

The plane surface mounted is advanced from the wall. The panel on its mount, the white ground on the panel, the paint on the white ground— everything is visible, nothing concealed. The painting is objectness and it is objectlessness. The "non-objectivity" presents the nature and order of colour and by it, nature (physis) is addressed.

Colour-shapes configure and reveal a necessity. Primary and primal realities unfold. No theory has been adhered to, no system imposed. If "system" is seen to evolve, it is the inherent necessity of matter and of vision. Generality becomes the particular; the particular, universal. Colour, as matter and light, declares its will to the willing viewer.

My art is visual, a perceptual realism of matter, of light, of dimension, of time— the phenomenon of colour.

July, 1986.

Point to Line to Plane. Drawings 1973 - 1985.

This exhibition of drawings is chosen from 13 years of my work. It makes visible the necessity of the elements in drawing and in painting. Point, the proto-element, and line, its extension, are parent to plane in both its active form (the shape) and its basic form (the page). Elements have energy and order and so they have meaning. Meaning is recognized in drawing and in painting by the simple act of *noticing*.

Point (the pen or pencil point) extended to line yields direction: horizontal, vertical, diagonal or oblique. The straight line on the plane (page) affirms the materiality of the plane and its two-dimensional nature.

Drawing (the act) begins with the size and shape of the page (plane). The order and energy of the size and shape of the plane are determining factors for the configuration on it. The square page and the square shape on the plane share order and energy of shape. The square shape repeated, packed and stacked on the plane, shares with the plane its size.

The contour of a square shape is horizontal and vertical. The square shape has two opposing diagonals. Four lines, four directions determine the form of the square shape. The form of the square shape is in accord always with its order and energy. All of this is real.

A square shape may be realized with lines in one direction. All horizontal, all vertical, or all diagonal lines in one or the other diagonal direction realize a square shape. Each line and all lines together achieve the plane of the square shape and reveal its energy. They affirm the order and energy of the shape and of the plane (page).

The lines yield a shape and this shape (the square shape) is a plane. The drawn shape is a plane shape, the same plane as the page. The lines, compacted or released, afford interrelated spaces between the lines; the shapes, compacted or released, afford interrelated spaces between the shapes; they create new energies, new shapes and renew order and energy.

Relationship depends on the shape and on the plane. Regular and irregular relationships depend on each other. Shapes relate to other shapes (regular), to spaces between shapes (irregular), and interdependence is complete. Shapes abut shapes making new shapes and "lines" for the eye. Position is an element in drawing.

Lines that are not horizontal, not vertical, not diagonal, but are oblique in relation to the plane (page) make new shapes of another (irregular) order. The irregular shape with three, or four, or five directions, is also a plane shape. Its form and order confirm the order and energy of the plane (page). All directions make the plane shape.

The plane shape is not ambiguous. It is not either one thing or the other, nor sometimes one thing or the other. The plane shape is *all these things*.

The graphite from the pencil (grey) and the ink from the pen (black) mark the plane (white). The grey stroke and its repetition determine value; the black line and its repetition determine density. The white (light) page is in greatest opposition and contrast to the grey stroke and the black line; it intensifies the darkness of each line and each shape. The white page mixes with the blackness of each shape to yield a flux of greys. Colour is an element in the drawing.

Time is an element of the work and in the work. Time, duration, is a factor in marking and making, and it is a factor in noticing. For the artist and for the viewer, time passes, and from the artist, time passes into the drawing. Point extends to line. Each line has direction. Each line has the direction of the shape and is directed by the plane. Time is a dimension in drawing. Time and line endure. In the drawing, each line and all lines sustain a synthesis *all of the time*.

In my drawings, the elements configure and reveal necessity; fundamental realities unfold. All this is visible for the conscious eye.

> ... not the smallest alteration in the nature, in the character, in the effects of the individual elements should escape the watchful eye.
>
> Wassily Kandinsky
>
> *Point and Line to Plane*, 1926

March, 1988

Working Notes and Drawings.

14 August, 1990. Tuesday

I completed the fourth drawing today. This is the fourth of four. I set aside this work now. I have been "playing," too. I've been playing with circles (discs?) drawn with parallel lines. The circles abut and at the point where they touch another direction of parallel lines begins drawn parallel to the point. The point is not a point because I have extended it to a line as if there had been "impact" where the shapes abut. The image grew out of the idea or search for a self-reference point upon which to build the planar circle. An interesting image and concept here, but I have nowhere to go with it.

16 August, 1990. Thursday

I am at an impasse with drawing. I believe I will set all aside now and go on with other things. I have made a small drawing (10" x 10") of drawn plane circles each abutting another one, another two, three, four or five. In this drawing, I seem to have said all I know to say. I have nowhere to go with it even though it (this idea and the realization of it by drawing) seems full of potential. Perhaps there is something I'm not seeing here, or it may be that the circle by nature is always closed and there is nowhere to go.

In my effort to clarify surface and shape using this figure (the circle has no straight edge and its curved circumference has no beginning or end), I found an answer that was self-referential, but at the same time it is as limiting as the figure itself. Each shape's surface begins and ends only in relation to the shape/surface that abuts it. There is nothing wrong with this; in fact, it seems a revelation in itself, but having realized [drawn] it, I see only the possibility of increasing the number of circles involved and that doesn't give me the direction or impetus I believe I need. Strange.

There are other good things inherent in this idea [drawing]. I draw circles abutting circles, large and small. The line drawn at the point where the circles touch serves to unify the plane. The tendency to regard large shapes as near and small shapes as farther away in illusory space is destroyed by that line at the point where the circles abut. This configuration of round shapes is entirely planar; the two-dimensionality of the plane is intact. More— it is emphasized in this unlikely image.

I don't see that I should proceed to a larger page. At this point, I could only repeat what I have found out. I don't believe I can find out more by using more (or fewer) circles on a larger page— not yet, anyway.

30 August, 1990. Thursday

I have been drawing since last writing here. At present, I'm cleaning my pen; I will go on drawing. I'm working on a small page (8" x 8"). I combine straight-edged [irregular] shapes (three, four and five-sided shapes whose surface is realized by drawing all lines parallel to their boundaries) and the large and small circles. All of the shapes abut and the surface of each circle is made by drawing all lines parallel to the abutting points. The "point" is indicated by a line which shows "contact" and gives clarity to what is happening on the page. The circles are not circles at all; rather, they are plane shapes, too. They have no boundary in the way the straight-edged shapes are bound. They have *energy* and all of that energy is generated by *contact*— that contact, then, creates their *surface*.

I have made three small drawings and have begun a fourth. I have six sketches and prepared six pieces of paper. I make these drawings so I can see them. Something important is happening here, but it is *small* and it is subtle.

1 September, 1990. Saturday

Phone call yesterday from Catherine Carmichael. She is putting together a show that will focus on "process" for the Extension Gallery at 80 Spadina. The point is not to show a completed work, but the preliminaries to it— notes, sketches, etc. Nice idea, but I'm not enthused about it. I'm pleased she thought of me for it.

I continue to draw. I'm at work on the sixth (last) small drawing.

2 September, 1990. Sunday.
Have put my pen in cleaner. The six small drawings are complete. I have tried to push on with round shapes, shapes without drawn boundaries—surface shapes. I seem to get nowhere.

The six drawings are fine for the eye and they tell themselves well. The bound shapes in them (three-sided, four-sided and five-sided shapes) create the surface of those shapes and give direction to the surface of the circles (discs?), or should I say the "unbound" shapes that abut the bound shapes gain surface from them. This is clear and *observable*. Each shape is the consequence of the energy generated by each other shape that abuts it, so the unbound shapes are *surfaces* of parallel lines (energy) in as many directions as there are points of contact with other shapes. How to say this in words?

Perhaps I can't move on this because I can't see it all yet. It does not open out as other thoughts sometimes do. There is an idea here and I cannot make it fly.

I've been drawing for weeks. I wash my pen and go on to other things. There is always so much to do.

Primal Colour Paintings.

Colour is the subject of my work— colour, its energy and activity. The surface is paint; that paint is colour. Colour, its interaction and interdependence is the subject and the meaning of my work.

In my paintings, colour takes precedence over form and generates the event of the work. Each work presents the primary and primal necessity of colour. Red, yellow and blue (primary) are at work; "black" and "white" (primal) interact with red, yellow and blue— relationship is manifest, interdependence effects phenomena.

From 1969 to 1983 I made the works that I call the *Colour Lock Paintings*. In these works, I explore (and make manifest) the energy of colour; I discover the necessities of redness, yellowness and blueness, and I am made cognizant of the primal nature of their relationship. I make colour-black, colour-grey and colour-white extend that relationship.

The *Colour Lock* paintings are acrylic on canvas, and they are large works. Their size is accordant with human stature and human vision. The paintings are planar; their configuration is orderly (horizontally and vertically disposed). In these works, colour and shape (colour-shape) are perceived as *one thing*.

In 1984 I began to make "small paintings." These works are acrylic on masonite panel, mounted on wood. They address "smallness," that particular of size, as an essential element. The plane surface, mounted, is advanced from the wall. The panel on its mount, the white ground on the panel, the paint on the white ground— everything is visible; nothing is concealed.

The small paintings are orderly and they are de-ordered. Five components (colour-shapes) create a new configuration in each work; new intermixtures of pigment yield new reds, new yellows, new blues, new blacks, new whites in each work. The painted plane is colour-active.

In 1986 I made the *Primal Colour Paintings*. In 1986 all that is past in my work becomes prologue and informs these paintings.

The 20 small paintings in this exhibition are *primal colour* paintings. I use the word "primal" when red, yellow and blue are intermixed to yield black. The black which is the consequence of the intermixture of the primary colours may favour redness, yellowness, or blueness, and it reflects that primary's energy and exercises its colour-action.

The colours red, yellow and blue (primary) intermix to yield orange, green and purple (binary). When two pigments are combined in intermixture, the resulting colour is reduced in colour-value; that is, it is *greyed*.

When blue is intermixed with red, the combination yields purple. Purple can be seen to be lower in dark/light value, and in colour-value, than either red or blue.

When red is intermixed with yellow, the resulting orange is said to be lower in value than yellow, but higher in value than red. This describes the dark/light value of orange in relation to red and yellow; it does not describe what I am calling "colour-value."

When red is intermixed with yellow, there is a loss of the intensity of both the red and the yellow in the resulting orange. The colour-value of that orange is reduced; it is *greyed*, or it can be said to be *proceeding toward black*.

All intermixtures of colour lose intensity, reduce in colour-value, and proceed toward black.

Black is the *primal* colour, an intermixture of red, yellow and blue, where each primary colour reduces each other primary colour until the primal state of colour (pigment) is achieved. By subtractive intermixture, colour returns to the darkness of the earth whence it comes.

The *Primal Colour Paintings* are red, yellow and blue. In them, "black" is primal, always made of red, yellow and blue; white is always a colour-white reflecting whiteness (light), interacting by hue; grey is primal black and white together. All is red, yellow and blue.

Colour-shapes configure; they order and de-order (re-order) the plane. Colour orders, shape de-orders, primary and primal energies unfold and four colour-shapes find equilibrium. The non-objective configuration presents the nature and order of colour, and by it, nature (physis) is addressed.

I made these paintings for a viewer (like me) who is open to the presence of colour, willing to be engaged by it and absorbed in its meaning.

To describe a painting in words is to rob it of its immediacy, but to not describe it risks the denial of its presence. I describe *Primal Black: Red* (9" x 10") using words which I believe report the presence and the action of that work.

The painting is composed of four colour-shapes. There is a vertical "black" shape at right which is separated from the other three colour-shapes by exposed white ground. White ground is exposed at the top edge of the panel. The white ground isolates the three colour-shapes and makes of them one shape, a square shape, which is placed (displaced) at the left of and lower than the vertical "black" shape on the panel. The vertical "black" shape is narrow and it is as tall as the panel (9"). It is a red-black, an intermixture of red, yellow and blue.

The square shape is bound by exposed white ground at top and right, and by the panel's edge at left and bottom. It is divided into three colour areas (colour-shapes) which abut— a blue shape, a red shape and a yellow shape.

The blue shape is a vertical at the left of the panel. It is wider than the "black" shape at the right and it shares a vertical boundary with the red shape that is at centre. The red shape is a quadrilateral which shares an oblique boundary with the yellow shape. The yellow shape is bound at its right edge by the exposed white ground. The relationship of the red shape and the yellow shape may be called inverse and opposite, or upside down and backwards. They are not equal. The centre quadrilateral (red) is the larger of the two.

The red shape is an intermixture of cadmium and crimson pigments— redness is whole and complete. The blue shape is ultramarine reduced by an intermixture of red, yellow and blue, that is, by the red-black of the vertical shape at the right of the panel. The yellow shape is the smallest of the three primary colour-shapes. An intermixture of yellow and red-black, it reduces to "green."

The red-black vertical shape at right and the reduced blue vertical shape at left are low in dark/light value. The blue maintains its identity of blueness (leaning toward purple) and the red-black shows its redness. These similar (vertical rectangles) but unequal shapes are in extreme positions at the left and right edges of the panel.

The red shape and the yellow ("green") shape are similar in dark/light value. Together they form a vertical rectangle. The red shape's intensity and the yellow shape's tendency to "green" (the complement of red) create a singular opposition between them, as does the eccentric and inclined shared boundary (the oblique).

The intense primary (red) is the largest colour-shape in the painting; the "black" shape is the smallest.

The painting has four shapes and four colours— four different shapes and four different colours. Each shape is vertically disposed on the panel and each extends left and right (horizontally) in colour relationship with each other shape. All of the colour-shapes reflect redness and all of them yield to reduction and proceed more or less toward black.

Again— the "black" shape reflects red; the blue shape (purple) approaches black; the yellow shape approaches "green" and it reflects blueness and redness. The red shape is *greyed*; it has, by its combination of cadmium and crimson, components of yellow and of blue. The character of each colour is beyond naming. The behaviour (action) of each colour-shape, and (interaction) of all colour-shapes together, is unnamable, but it is evident, self-evident, self-generating and it persists in time.

I cite this painting with words. All that I cite is real and it is happening. In words, the description is long and linear and is separated in time. In the painting, event happens all together, all at once, and it is happening all of the time.

September, 1991

Colour / Shape / Surface: small paintings and drawings 1987-88.

In this post-modern age, it has become common practice for a written text to accompany an exhibition of visual art. It is important, however, that what is written act as a guide for the viewer and that it not be misleading. Visual art that is about perception requires looking, noticing, seeing and knowing what one is seeing. These things, not what is written on a page, best inform the viewer.

My work has been called "abstract," "minimal," "formalist" and sometimes "geometric." These adjectives don't describe my work; instead, they place it in categories where it does not belong. My work is not "abstract"; rather, it is *concrete*. It is not "minimal" because it is highly active with colour and with shape; while my work shows an *economy*, no more and no less than its necessity, it does not meet the criteria for minimalism. What have now become the conventions of "formalism" can be applied only loosely to my work. The word "geometric" refers to shape; specifically, it describes the contour of a shape. In my paintings, shapes have surface; they are colour-active and they are not about geometry. I reject these adjectives as generalizations which classify my work in someone else's past and lead the viewer away from what is present in the work onto paths of memory and recall, or academe.

Words are about *naming*. To write about my work I must use words, names which report what is seen. Words are metaphors for perceived realities; I will try to use words that emphasize what is perceived, what is real. I prefer to use the word "non-objective" to describe my work, giving that word the same meaning that Malevich gave it. The painting is an object, but it is non-objective; that is, it *presents* phenomena, it does not *represent* an object seen in space. I choose the word *concrete* to describe material presence in the same way Barnett Newman did. I believe *concrete painting* is about colour interaction as Josef Albers did. *Painters paint paint and that paint is coloured.* Colour, shape and surface are real and self-evident on the plane; as matter and as light, they create a visual phenomenon for the willing viewer.

Since 1984, I have been exploring irregular shape in my paintings and in my drawings. The shape of the plane is ordered (a square, a rectangle); the shapes on the plane are irregular and they de-order (re-order) the plane. The de-ordered plane is a chaos. Irregular shapes determine the "order" of that chaos.

For this exhibition, I have chosen small paintings and drawings made in 1987-88. These works have not been exhibited previously, and the Blackwood Gallery offers me an opportunity to show them as individual works (each work is complete in itself) and as an installation (seen together they show a progression of my concern with the irregular).

I will write about these works in three sections. What I write can be seen by anyone (everyone) who is willing to look. I encourage the reader to stop reading so s/he might look; I suggest that the viewer notice everything that is real and visible even if I have not written about it. The viewer's experience is one of seeing, and of knowing what s/he is seeing.

5 small paintings

Size is an element in painting. In these works, I explore the dimension of smallness, that particular of size, and by it, I explore the painting as object and as surface. The plane surface, mounted, is advanced from the wall. The panel on its mount, the white ground on the panel, the paint on the white ground— everything is visible, nothing concealed.

These small paintings are about colour and shape, and about the position of each colour shape on the plane. Each work has two colours and two shapes, and the two colour-shapes occupy the entire surface. The two colour-shapes are delineated by each other and by the boundary of the plane. Each colour-shape is an irregular plane shape.

The two irregular colour-shapes co-operate on the plane. They are separated from each other by exposed white ground. One colour-shape "surrounds" the other. The "surround" shape is separated from the boundary of the plane by exposed white ground; its position is shifted up, down or across the two-dimensional plane. The two colours are analogous; they interact by gentle opposition.[1] The necessity of shape is interrelationship; the necessity of colour is interdependence.

16 drawings

These drawings are selected from two separate, but related, groups of works.[2] The first series of drawings has irregular shapes drawn upon the plane separated from one another. The white page shape surrounds each drawn shape. In the second series of drawings, the same irregular shapes are drawn upon the plane abutting one another. The white page shape surrounds the abutted drawn shapes as one shape on the plane. New energies are at work in each drawing. Samenesses confront differences as drawn shapes configure with the white page shape.

In these drawings, each shape's surface is made of all lines drawn parallel to all of its boundaries. Each surface differs in relation to the boundary and the surface of a shape drawn in the first series differs from the surface of that same shape drawn again in the second series. Time is in evidence and it is an element in these drawings.

The drawn shapes are irregular plane shapes— three-sided, four-sided, five-sided and six-sided shapes. A shape's surface, then, is drawn in three, four, five or six directions. The surface is densest and darkest where the greatest number of directions have been drawn. The white page reflects light from the interstices between the drawn lines and black is modulated to grey creating nuances of blacks and greys. Black, grey and white are colours; the drawing's energy and action are a *colour-action* of contrasts between the irregular drawn shapes and the white page shape, and between each irregular drawn shape and another. All of this is visible and it is happening altogether, all of the time.

4 untitled paintings

In these paintings, three-sided, four-sided, five-sided and six-sided irregular colour-shapes occupy the plane. Exposed white ground separates the colour-shapes. Where the white ground is a narrow shape, colour-shapes collect and together separate from the colour-shape bound by a wider white ground shape. The exposed white ground at the boundary of the plane gives another boundary to the colour-shapes and positions them up, down or leftward, rightward on the plane. Position is composition.[3]

Red, yellow and blue occur in each painting. These colours are primary and they are primal (reduced by intermixture). Each "red" is a new red; each "blue" and each "yellow" is new. The combinations of colours and the juxtapositions of shapes, together manifest relatedness and create interaction. Each painting, complete, has a particular interdependence. Colour, as light, is reflected from the painted plane.

I have written these words so the viewer can make a beginning free of memory and history in the presence of my paintings and drawings. I have not said what the viewer should think or feel about my work; rather, my words tell (name) what is real and present and visible.

November, 1993

Notes:

1. The analogous colour relationship in each painting is also expressed in its title: *Yellow and Yellow-Orange* (9" x 9"); *Red and Red-Purple* (10" x 10"); *Blue and Blue-Green* (10" x 12"); *Red and Red-Orange* (12" x 14"); *Blue and Blue-Purple* (12" x 14").

2. Of the 16 drawings, eight were chosen from *Surface/Boundary, Series 1;* the eight companion works were chosen from *Surface/Boundary, Series 2*. All of the drawings are ink on paper; all are 15" x 15".

3. The four paintings are: *Untitled #1 1988*; *Untitled #4 1988*; *Untitled #5 1988; Untitled #6 1988*. All are acrylic on panel mounted on wood; all are 20" x 20".

Paintings 1990-91 and Drawings 1984 & 1990.

Since 1984, I have been working with irregular shapes in my paintings and in my drawings. Over these years, my understanding of the de-ordered surface has evolved through the works I have produced. Each work is a *question*; it addresses the behaviour of irregular relationships. Each work is the *answer* to its own question; through irregular shapes and relationships (chaos), a new "order" occurs.

My earlier work, the *Colour Lock Paintings* (1969-1983), is often called "formalist." If this word is descriptive of it, then my work since 1984 should be called "post-formalist." Using the elements of size, shape and surface, line and colour, their interaction and interdependence, my paintings and drawings *deconstruct* what is understood, by convention, to be "formalist" in them without destroying the action and energy of the elements, that is, without compromise. My intent is not to violate the creative act, but to confirm it by pursuing it, extending it and preserving it in a new form.

I do not speak of transcendence, the metaphysical or the spiritual in relation to my work. Instead, I emphasize what is real, concrete and visible. It is the engagement of the eye and mind with what is perceived that stokes the will to art, that fires the artist to make art, and warms the viewer who receives it. This is a fundamental human act on both sides of the equation, and it is the only ground on which the artist and the viewer are equal.

I believe that however difficult it is to describe or define the experience of visual sensation and perception, it is by these means, and these means alone, that people respond to paintings. My work is about colour and the perception of it; my work is phenomenological and experiential.

In this exhibition, I have brought together drawings and paintings which explore irregular shapes. These works, made in 1984 and in 1990-91, show the beginning and the development of my work with the irregular. All of these works are planar. The shape of the plane is orderly (a square, a rectangle); the shapes on the plane are irregular and they de-order (re-order) the plane.

The six *Plane Shape* drawings exhibited here were made in 1984.[1] They are among the earliest works in which I involved an irregular shape. In them, the square page, the square shape on the page and the irregular quadrilateral shape are each (all) planar. Each drawing combines the same shapes; each work is drawn with lines in different directions, or new combinations of directions. There are eight directions inherent in these shapes. In these drawings, line (direction) creates surface and new irregular shapes.

From this beginning where one irregular shape behaves in co-operation with orderly shapes, I increased the number of irregular shapes and relationships in my drawings and in my paintings. I made and exhibited my *Small Paintings* (1984-5) and *Primal Colour Paintings* (1986) and I made many, many drawings. In making drawings, I found a latitude that gave me the freedom to explore new relationships. The drawings, *Surface/Boundary, Series 1* and *Surface/Boundary, Series 2* (1987), were a culmination of my search for the order of wholly irregular relationship on the square plane. The plane, de-ordered, is a chaos; irregular shape and relationship determines the order of that chaos.

The two drawings, *One Plane/Eleven Drawn Shapes #1* and *One Plane/Eleven Drawn Shapes #2*, were made in 1990[2] just prior to the paintings in this exhibition. In them, all of the drawn shapes are irregular and all are planar. Each shape's surface is realized by drawing all lines parallel to each shape's boundary. Each surface differs in relation to the boundary of the shape. The drawn shapes are three-sided, four-sided, five-sided and six-sided. A shape's surface, then, is drawn in three, four, five or six directions. The white page reflects light from the interstices between the drawn black lines, and black is modulated to greys. Black, grey and white are colours; the drawing's action includes a *colour-action* in the contrasts between the irregular drawn shapes and the white page that surrounds and separates them. The shape of the page, a rectangle, is the only orderly shape in each work. It is the white page that is de-ordered (re-ordered) by the action of the irregular shapes on it. The white page is as integral to the configuration as are the shapes on it.

The paintings in this exhibition are about irregular colour-shapes on a coloured ground.[3] In them, colour takes precedence over form and generates the event of the work. The colour-shapes are three-sided, four-sided and five-sided and all are planar; that is, they are two-dimensional colour surfaces that lie on the two-dimensional surface of the coloured canvas ground. The size of each shape gives its colour a particular value; the shape of each colour gives that colour a particular energy. The irregular colour-shapes and the shape of the coloured ground that surrounds and separates them configure and co-operate. By interaction and interdependence (necessity), the irregular colour-shapes de-order and re-order the plane and a new order occurs.

Colour exerts an energy that excites the eye and mind. The eye receives (recept), the mind is engaged (percept), and the emotions are aroused. In this way, we *see* colour, we *know* that we are seeing it, and we say that we *respond* to it. This is perception. In painting, the event of colour arrests the eye; the phenomenon of colour activates the work and the mind of the viewer who is open to it.

24 April, 1996

Notes:

1. The size of the *Plane Shape* drawings is 15" x 15".

2. The size of the two 1990 drawings is 22.5" x 28".

3. Nine paintings, acrylic on canvas, were shown; three of them were 42" x 48", four were 48" x 54" and two were 48" x 96".

Serial Works: paintings and drawings.

My paintings are about colour, its energy and activity, its interaction and interdependence. My drawings are about the elements that constitute the work: line, direction, shape and surface. My work is "abstract" or non-objective, and it is rigorously planar.

The works in this exhibition present forms of seriality. In each series, the works can be viewed separately, in groups within the series, and ultimately as a series of interrelated works that together continue and complete each other to become one work.

The Paintings.

On Redness #1-4, *On Yellowness #1-4* and *On Blueness #1-4* are three works, each consisting of four paintings.[1] Each of the three series is focused on a primary colour. The four paintings in each series sustain a primary colour in four variations as coloured canvas grounds. The relationships of the colour-shapes on the coloured ground to each other in each painting are as vital as the relationships of the colour-shapes, both as colour and as shape, between the four paintings in each serial work. The works were made to emphasize a particular aspect of the serial and were the consequence of the body of work that preceded them.

Chronologically, the seven small *Eureka* paintings are the earliest paintings in this exhibition.[2] They are single, separate works, not a "series." Seen together here, they show a consistency of purpose by which I pursued a diversity of colour and shape. In each painting, four shapes create two more highly irregular plane shapes; one is at centre, the other is a "surround" shape. These paintings grew out of an earlier approach taken in drawings that failed and that I have abandoned. The change from line (drawing) to *colour* (painting) clarified what I was after and gave impetus to the works that followed. The title of these seven small paintings reflects the breakthrough I believed I had made.

Three paintings, *On Redness (red and blue)*, *On Yellowness (yellow and red)* and *On Blueness (blue and yellow)* followed the *Eureka* paintings. They were made as single works, but their colour, that is, the primary relationships within each and between the three paintings, have made them a group or series: three paintings as one work.[3]

The three series of four paintings described above are the outcome of these 10 paintings. In them, six colour-shapes reduce to five, to four, then to three colour-shapes on a primary ground. All is red, yellow and blue.

The Drawings.

Configuring #1-9.[4] In this series, each drawing is complete in itself. The white page and the irregular shapes drawn on the page are in interaction. The surface of each shape is drawn with lines in directions relevant to its boundary. Each shape's surface is particular and integrates the white of the paper. The series shows a relatedness that turns similarity into difference. The drawings may be viewed singly or in groups of three, but it is as a series of nine that an essential constancy and continuation is realized and completed.

In *Van Doesburg's Alphabet* only horizontal, vertical and diagonal lines are drawn. Each letter form is a square and I have drawn the square-shape to co-operate with the square plane of the paper. The serial aspect of these works depends on the alphabet itself. The letters from A to Z are in their traditional positions. The series of drawings is understood by the serial form of the alphabet— each letter is separate from each other letter; each is defined by the letter that precedes it and follows it, but the series is complete only when all 26 drawings are present. For this reason, I have included *Van Doesburg's Alphabet* in this exhibition.[5]

Van Doesburg's Alphabet[6]

Theo van Doesburg (1883-1931) is a seminal figure in modern art. With Piet Mondrian, he was co-founder and editor of *De Stijl*. His art encompassed painting, architecture, writing, philosophy, typography and design.

In 1919, Van Doesburg created an alphabet of letters built on the square using only the horizontal and the vertical. This alphabet is simple, orderly and beautiful. I have used Van Doesburg's alphabet as the subject of a series of drawings.

Van Doesburg's Alphabet is a collection of 26 drawings, each presenting a letter of the 1919 alphabet. The drawings are made with lines drawn in four directions: the horizontal, the vertical and the two diagonals. I have drawn the square shape that each letter occupies on a page proportional to it. The energy and inherent logic of each letter directed its position on the page. Each letter is a generative device; the drawings are about the square and the directions of lines that define it. The drawings were made in 1981.

There are 22 paintings and 36 drawings in this exhibition. They occur as single works and as serial works and are shown here in that manner. The extraordinary space of the Artword Gallery has allowed me to present groups of works as one work as well as to show the chronological development that led to their realization.

October, 1999

Notes:

1. The 12 paintings in the three series are each 15" x 15". They are acrylic on canvas; they were made in 1992.
2. The *Eureka* paintings are 10" x 10". They are acrylic on canvas; they were made in 1992.
3. The three paintings in this series are each 15" x 15". They are acrylic on canvas; they were made in 1992.
4. The nine drawings in this series are each 15" x 15". They are ink on paper; they were made in 1993.
5. The 26 drawings in *Van Doesburg's Alphabet* are each 9" x 9"; they are ink on paper.
6. This descriptive text was posted on a wall of the gallery near the alphabet drawings.

Reds, Yellows, Blues, Blacks and Whites.

Viewers who saw my show *Serial Works* in 1999 at Artword Gallery will recognize a continuation in aspects of the work in this exhibition. Again, groups of paintings constitute one work and other paintings are individual works. The drawings, each a separate, individual work, were made in a series to explore, sustain and exhaust their potential.

The paintings in this exhibition are about colour contrast— high and low contrasts of value and of hue. This is expressed in the title of each work.[1] There are three series of paintings, each consisting of three paintings; each series constitutes one work. In each series, a primary colour contrasts with colour-whites, colour-blacks and its own primary nature. Each work has seven shapes, *centre* shapes and *surround* shapes. These shapes increase and decrease in number on the primary coloured grounds as each series progresses.

Another three paintings, each an individual work, are separate from, but related to, the three serial works. In them, primary colours contrast with each other on primary coloured grounds.

The paintings were made in 1993-94.

The drawings were made in 1991. Each drawing is complete in itself. The white paper and the shapes drawn on the paper interact. The surface of each shape is drawn with lines parallel to its boundary; each shape's surface is particular and integrates the white of the paper. The white page (plane) that surrounds and separates each shape is an integral part of the work. In making my drawings, I work the whole page and I frame them accordingly.

In the drawings, the white ground (paper) is an active shape. I exposed the energy of that shape as I laid drawn shapes on each page. As in the paintings, the ground shape co-operates with the applied shapes in each work as new shape and new colour.

The 12 paintings[2] and 21 drawings[3] in this show have not been exhibited previously.

September, 2000

Notes:

1. As an example, the three paintings in the "red" series are titled *Red on Red and Whites*, *Red on Red and Blacks* and *Red on Red and Reds*. The three paintings in the "yellow" series, and those in the "blue" series are similarly titled.

2. The 12 paintings are each 20" x 20"; they are acrylic on canvas.

3. The drawings, *One Plane/Configuration #1-21*, are each 15" x 15"; they are ink on paper.

Some Letters (1987-1991)

Letter to a Young Canadian Sculptor.

(Excerpt from a letter to a sculptor doing post-graduate work in England.)

2 December, 1987.

Dear ______

I don't think I was much help to you during that phone call. The problems you're having in relocating your work place, finding sources for materials, meeting new people— all of them with different approaches to making art and one of whom is supposed to be giving you some direction— all of it is frustrating and until you get a handle on some of this, it's depressing. If I tell you not to be depressed, not to let the frustrations get you down, it will sound like so many empty words, or it will seem so until you are up about something. Then you will know what I mean, but you'll say: "Of course, I knew that all along."

Your greatest problem (in your own estimation) is that you feel lost with your own work. You want to dig in, get something going, but you don't quite know what to do. What you've decided to do doesn't seem good enough and you don't know how to make it better, and you're thinking that maybe you should be doing something entirely different! (I know from experience that this is the height of frustration and the pits of depression.)

So, how can a person proceed feeling like that? Well, I have a little ploy that has worked for me in the past, and it may be of some use to you. I call it GOING THROUGH THE MOTIONS. Mind, you have to be awfully depressed, at wit's end, to need this ploy. It is simply what it says. Go through the motions making something: a drawing, a painting, a sculpture, or a few sketches toward an idea for a painting or a sculpture. Forget for a while that there is anything at stake. Put something down, marking a page, laying down ideas that aren't really ideas at all— they are an excuse to *go through the motions*. If you have something started, but you've lost faith in it, keep working on it bearing in mind that there is nothing at stake because you are simply GOING THROUGH THE MOTIONS.

Now, this doesn't mean that you are working idly, or that you are not thinking as you work. You will have to think about what you're doing just to *go through the motions*, but ask nothing more than that of yourself. Carry through the work— if it is a piece of sculpture, you'll want to accomplish the best piece of *mediocre* sculpture you physically know how to do; if it's a drawing, put down your *poor* ideas as carefully as you can so you can feel proud of the *unimaginative* work you have done. Or put down something you already know you can handle. If it seems unworthy, get it down anyway. Once you have carried something through, keep it around. You'll need to look at it to assess the real measure of your success or failure with the work. You must be a good judge of how well or how poorly you have done this task of GOING THROUGH THE MOTIONS.

In my experience, this ploy prompts new ideas. Don't stop what you're doing to go on to something that seems better. Make some notes about the new idea so you won't lose it, but don't quit on the first work to start work on the new idea. If you have a flood of ideas, sketch them out before they dissipate (or else later, you won't be able to remember even one good idea when you want it), but keep working on the piece at hand.

All this will sound pretty stupid. Go ahead and tell yourself that it's stupid, but don't abandon the work because of that. Later, when you can do no more on the work, you may conclude that it is a pretty well-handled STUPID sculpture, or a STUPID drawing, but you have to go through all the motions first so you can see if that's true.

It is better to make a poor piece of work than no work at all. *Something* will have been accomplished by it. It's better to *go through the motions* than to fret about what's not happening for you in your work. It's a bit like the lottery; you can't win if you don't buy a ticket, but with GOING THROUGH THE MOTIONS, chances are a lot better for you. You will be *making something happen* no matter how poor it is and if it is a real disaster, you can try again and make it better. When you are at this point (where *critical judgement* comes into play), you are on your way to *somewhere*.

Because you are working with other students, they will probably want to know what you are doing. You can tell them that you are GOING THROUGH THE MOTIONS. You won't have to explain this to them because there isn't much to explain. If they ask what you intend with the work you are doing, answer that you haven't found out yet and keep going. Or, if you want to talk it up with them, tell them whatever bullshit you want, but YOU know that you are GOING THROUGH THE MOTIONS, and YOU know that there is *nothing at stake*.

If your instructor has some suggestions about the work, listen carefully. You may not do what he suggests, or you may want to try it. It is important to listen, however, because the instructor is giving you *his thinking* about the work at hand and there may be something useful in it, not for *this* work, but for some future work. You don't have to follow instructions when you are GOING THROUGH THE MOTIONS, because you don't need them. You already know what you're doing— you are GOING THROUGH THE MOTIONS, and there is nothing at stake.

The best part of this ploy is that sometimes you will end with a good piece of work. It won't be great, but it will be good. It may show more potential than you thought it could. It will be good for you to see that, because, remember, you were only going through the motions. Often, this ploy sparks a flood of ideas, particularly if you are drawing, or sketching toward a painting or a sculpture. When you are good at going through the motions, you'll be able to get down every one of those ideas in some form. They will be good ideas and poor ones, some worth further work, some not worth bothering with. You can deal with them later when your *critical judgement* is at work. Get them down on paper, made concrete, and you'll have something to play with even if they don't go anywhere. Getting things down in concrete form is very important— bad sketches, stupid drawings, mediocre forms, dumb ideas— all are worth making concrete so you can abandon them later when you bring *critical judgement* into play. Do you remember those lines from my essay: "The stuff of the mind is not the stuff of paint" and "I have to make it so I can see it"? An idea is of no use to a visual artist until it is made concrete. Only then can the worth of the idea be assessed. One must not shrink from one's own crummy ideas. Get them down, *then* decide how crummy they are and go on from there.

Some people bring *critical judgement* into play *before* they have made anything concrete. They think their thoughts, then abandon them without putting them down to look at them. This is a mistake. Put them down, even if you are only going through the motions, *then* assess them, but not before. Honing one's critical faculty and refining one's vision are a large part of making art well. It can't happen without looking a lot and having a lot to look at— especially a lot of your own work, good, bad and indifferent.

Sometimes you will only have to go through the motions for a day and because you made something (in spite of yourself), you will suddenly be *on track*. Or, you may have to push away at it for a week. It's wise to keep every scrap of paper, every crummy drawing, painting or sketch (if you are carving wood, keep the wood chips), because they are *vital evidence* of what you are doing. Whenever you are going through the motions, and you *know* that's what you're doing, it's important that you lose nothing, not because it's all so creative and good, but because IT'S ALL YOU'VE GOT.

I discovered this ploy while I was a student. I got tired of telling myself: "I don't know what I'm doing." I devised this way of *knowing* what I was doing—I was GOING THROUGH THE MOTIONS. It gave me something to look at and I COULD SEE WHAT I HAD DONE. If I was unhappy with it, I could go on from there. Now, I rarely use this ploy directly, but I still puddle around looking for things in my roughest ideas. I put things down to get rid of the garbage in my head, then push that stuff around to see if there's the seed of something useful in it. As a student, I had to abandon judgements about what I was doing to keep doing. Now, I keep my critical faculty alive no matter what I'm doing—I have nothing to fear. As a student, you can sometimes feel overburdened by judgements— your own, your teacher's and your peers'. You can feel overwhelmed by the fact that people have been making art since time began, and all of it is better than anything you are able to do. This becomes demoralizing, but it's about expectations, your own and other people's. If you think about it, you can't do much with expectations; if the world should end tomorrow, an expectation isn't worth a damn, is it. Doing is now, and if the world ends tomorrow, you will have done something! If you can't think of anything else to do than going through the motions, then do that. Now is your chance; don't miss it.

Think about the "struggling" artist in light of your present frustrations. (Artists don't struggle because they have too little money; they usually find some way to cope with that.) It is the struggle to make and do, to find one's relevance through one's own art, to recognize one's worth when one has made something *worthy*— this is the real struggle. It is a long struggle because all of the art of history is precedent for whatever we do. We can't expect to make GREAT ART without absorbing something of all that has passed before us. (Happily, it is still present.) As we struggle with our own work, we work our way through paths that were opened by others to reach a new place where we know we have *something to add*.

You are finding Barbara Hepworth's sculptures a good experience; you said you were attracted to the use of "holes" in her works. Think about this; work it through *on her behalf*. Do it to learn what *she* was doing and why she was doing it, so you will *understand* a Hepworth sculpture. It will be a great experience and you will gain tremendously by it. It will inform your own work.

You will see a lot of work that is hard to understand. I do. But see it and think about it— even try to rethink it by making sketches of it. If the artist you are seeing has been struggling for years, has broken through, remember that you can't expect to grasp in only a few moments all that she has worked so long and hard to achieve. You know by now that art may be simple, but it is never easy.

I have written this crazy letter because I couldn't find the perfect thing to say to you on the phone on Saturday. I suspect I have not found it in all these pages, but I'll send this to you anyway as my best shot.

Barbara

Letters to a Scholar.

(Excerpts from letters to a Ph.D. candidate in Art History.)

6 December, 1988.

Dear ______
Give A. my regards when you see her. Let me remind you of something said during your visit here that you may want to mull over together. In the restaurant over lunch, A. described Dada as an anti-art that ran against the aesthetic of its time. Then, you asked me which Dada artist interested me and I said Jean Arp. Both of you said that Jean Arp's work wasn't *really* Dada. I'm aware that Arp's work may not fit into the art historian's definition of Dada, but I remind you that Arp was a co-founder of Dada in Zurich.

Am I to understand that in the context of "dada," Arp is somehow wrong? Can it be that the definition of Dada is wrong? Would the historian's definition change if Arp were included? Let me know your thoughts on this.

Barbara

5 January, 1989.

Dear ______
I must have written a very poor letter. I think you have misunderstood what I was saying.

Re: Dada/dada. Thank you for defining "the commonly used sense of the derivative adjective 'dada'" as opposed to "the historical term 'Dada.'" It was not too complicated for me, but I think you did not see the point I tried to raise.

You classified Arp's poetry as "dada," but said that his visual art was not "a typical representative of its [dada's] spirit"— a *typical* art historian's response. I accept the classifications of historical (Dada) and aesthetico-philosophical (dada) artists, but I'll still point out that neither the movement nor the spirit of the movement was invented by art historians. On the contrary, Dada was made by the artists, all of whom were "dada" in the aesthetic sense. The historian's definition, which has become a convention, fails. If Dada/dada is defined leaving Arp's visual art out of it, then there is something wrong with the definition!

I hope this zeroes in on the question I raised in my last letter.

Barbara

Letter to a Poet.

(Excerpts.)

5 May, 1990.

Dear ______

... your letter about your visits to galleries in London... Your descriptions of the works you saw are of great interest to me. A young artist friend has written to me already about the Arshile Gorky retrospective at Whitechapel Gallery. (Do you know that it's possible these days for a Canadian artist, graduated from university studies over the past decade, to know nothing about Gorky?)

Your account of Gorky's work through the 1920s and 1930s... Let me argue with the implications of this idea of "influence." Jackson Pollock said that American artists had to work their way *through* cubism. Pollock was being critical of those painters he believed were ignoring, rather than *working through*, modernist forms. By your own account, Gorky's work was not influenced; rather, he knew and understood modernist painting and was *working through* it. When influence is used to mean imitation [as it is with Gorky], it says that the artist is beating the bushes *behind* him, rather than those in front. Like a trail-blazer, the artist is trying to move ahead into unopened territory. If the path he is on has had others on it, he will work his way through it (it will inform him) to reach what he will know eventually is virgin ground.

When I read your line, "he adopts and adapts the possibilities of Cubism... Surrealism... and eventually, aspects of Abstract Expressionism," I made this margin note: "Gorky *is* abstract expressionism." Because Gorky died in 1948, he is often not included among the "first generation" of abstract expressionists. From what I know of his work (and your account of the show at Whitechapel would confirm this), Gorky bridges European modernism and the American AbEx movement in a very important way. He is neither a Surrealist nor wholly an abstractionist, but without his particular vision, AbEx may not have occurred. Historians give the flame to Pollock; I believe Gorky's hand was on it, too.

I am always disturbed by the tags that are put on Gorky's paintings. In discussions of Gorky's work, cubism means only Picasso and Surrealism means only Miró. [I don't dispute that he championed these two artists, but I don't believe he imitated them.] When cubist painting and Surrealist painting are reduced to one artist each, the definition is too narrow to say what modernist painting achieved. If we must classify painters by similarities of appearance to other painters, I wonder why Gorky is not compared to Kandinsky.

Gorky's "failure" (you must have known you would get me with *that* word) seems to rest on the fact that he remained a figurative painter (re: the portraits), even while he was working in an abstract manner. It seems that art historians believe that there are two separate streams in art— figurative and abstract— and they cannot be reconciled. Some artists believe this, too, and are critical of it (words like "semi-abstract" help to cloud the issue). Comments by Canadian artists, like "The subject doesn't matter" (L.L. FitzGerald) and "I look for the empty subject" (David Milne) go unexamined and these painters continue to be called "landscape" painters. I have not seen anyone ask of the FitzGerald quote:— if the subject doesn't matter, then what does?— or question the meaning of Milne's "*empty* subject." To my mind, both are saying that they are not painting *subjects*, they are making paintings. I wish I knew how to make that distinction clear, for it is the insight that revolutionized painting over the past century.

You may agree with me; you described Gorky's figurative works as "never *just* that." Your descriptions of certain paintings by title made my eyes hang out to see them.

Your visit to the Turner wing at the Tate recalled my visit in 1971 and your response to what you saw seemed much like my own. I was thunder-struck by Turner's late work, and it made me return to the earlier works.

I can see now one of the 1840s paintings in my mind and I suspect that it is the work with thick yellow and white paint that you described. The light from that painting leaps to the eye; I remember thinking what a grand experience it must have been for Turner when he saw what he had made. Turner is a fine example of a painter who knows that he paints paint and that it is colour. Some of his paintings are as modern as a Malevich and as alive as a Matisse.

I have followed you through the Tate from the Lucian Freud paintings, the Newman, Still and Rothko paintings to the cubist works of Picasso and Braque with images flashing on the screen of my mind. I enjoyed the tour. I'm much in tune with the art that most interests you. Your whole letter was a great read for me.

I have not read Rosalind Krauss' *The Myth of the Avant-Garde*. You seem surprised at the "conservative" thinking in art criticism. The reaction against what you've called "experimental" (you included bp) is not new, but it has blossomed into a new form under the umbrella of post-modern criticism. Concrete poetry and what I call *concrete painting* are considered experiments that failed— they have no meaning. Of course, I strongly disagree with this.

Through the 1980s there has been emphasis on popular culture, on figurative and anecdotal painting, paintings that depict social and political issues; this art has become mainstream. Critics love it because it is more literary than visual. They apply post-modern literary theory to it and there is no end to their theoretical inventions. This criticism is now of greater importance than the art that it addresses, and *that* has encouraged artists to become followers of its trends. Artists are behaving like groupies, following the critics to learn what is "new." What is "new" these days, is *old*. Artists are beating the bushes *behind* them.

Neo-expressionism took its cue from the German movement; Art Brut looked at graffiti; Pop art has been exploited shamelessly. Neo-geo pretends to have the discipline of "geometric" art (Mondrian), *and meaning* (a square is a house, a line is a road, and colour— migod!— is symbolic). Some artists imitate the appearance of surfaces and call their work "simulationist"; some imitate other art by repainting other artists' pictures, or by photographing them and incorporating them into their work to prove that the original is without integrity. Artists in the mainstream are attacking or exploiting the art of their fellows and the art of the past to show that meaning is arbitrary—a function of the mind of the viewer.

In art and art criticism, deconstruction has been used as a battering ram. I see nothing wrong with revision in art and literary criticism, but to only denigrate what one did not understand in the first place is absurd. Ergo—those awful critical biographies you mentioned.

I rail against these attitudes and find myself arguing with some of my friends. B. is steeped in post-structuralist deconstruction and it puts me at odds with his ideas about painting. His concerns are with writing, but these ideas are being cast over painting to obliterate its visual meaning and to articulate a literary meaning invented for it by the new critics. I don't blame B. for this, but he has more sympathy for this form of criticism than I do. My friend C., who is doing a doctorate in art history, has taken this form of criticism to heart. Before he began his studies, he responded to painting as a perceptual event and would have examined it in terms of vision. Now, he takes an intellectual approach—he examines himself in terms of psychology and transfers his understanding to the works. The problem this raises is pretty clear to me: the artist cannot be doing anything more than the viewer is able to grasp *before* he sees the work; therefore, seeing the work cannot, will not inform him. Instead, the viewer *re*-forms the work to conform to his preconceptions. The artist is effectively eliminated. Is this a worthy consequence of "intentional fallacy"?

I ask myself every other day if I have become some sort of reactionary, too! The art and art criticism of the past decade have put me in this odd position. I think we should stop calling abstract art and concrete poetry "experimental." Let's call it what it is: *advanced*. It is made real and meaningful by those with a consciousness that is advanced. The art they made was not some sort of experiment; it *works* by its own *necessity*. (Damn! I can't make words say what I want them to.)

Necessity = [inherent] need to be so.

You asked what I think of Barnett Newman's painting, *Voice of Fire*, and the controversy surrounding the purchase. The whole business distresses me, particularly the newspaper and radio coverage. Popular opinion is given the highest status on this matter. Informed and uninformed opinion are equal; one doesn't have to know what one is talking about to have an opinion. If I can get my head together, I will write about this in "A Letter from Paris" for *Work Seen*.

Barbara

Letters to a Literary Critic.

(Excerpts.)

7 August, 1991.

Dear ______

... I'll be at a terrible disadvantage. I'm a painter, not a writer. I know that it's because I'm a painter that you want me to read what you will write about painting, but how will I tell you about "the unnamable" in painting when I think you have missed it?

Okay. Send me your ideas, your comments, your pages, your chapters— I will read them and reply. Only in the friendliest manner will I try to wrestle you to the ground— win or lose, your project seems a good place to carry on our dialogue. Surely, we agree on something or we would not take such pleasure in seeing the same works of art.

I'm enclosing some paragraphs that I wrote in response to your letter. They are fragments, but they may be relevant. If nothing else, they will assure you that I do not take your project lightly.

For ______ 12 July, 1991.

You say you want to develop an analogy between linear perspective in painting and grammatical syntax in language. It seems to me that the modern period is an unlikely time for this. The development of linear perspective and grammatical syntax predate the modern period; they are not modernist.

If the analogy is to be between cubism and concrete poetry, these aspects of painting and of language are of little significance because cubism is not about linear perspective and it is not about the distortion of linear perspective. So, too, I suspect that concrete poetry is not about grammatical syntax or the destruction of it.

I think there is an important parallel between cubist painting and concrete poetry. Each is about a new consciousness or vision. In painting, what is given is that vision; in poetry, what is given is that consciousness—meaning resides in the work. The work must be grasped, pure and simple. The work presents conscious perception; it is about that; it occurred because of that; it is that.

The consequence of cubist painting was that it opened eyes to an art that was not constricted by the model of linear perspective (and concrete poetry opened minds to meaning in language that was not confined to grammatical syntax). Neither the painters nor the poets were motivated by these earlier models, nor did they want to distort or destroy them. It is true that perspective has been affected by cubist painting and syntax has been affected by concrete poetry insofar as *something was added* to the concept (context) of painting and of poetry.

A method of criticism is to make comparisons. If a critic compares cubist painting to earlier models, he is likely to miss the new meaning in the work. He pulls the new into the old model; he superimposes what is old onto what is new and marks off the differences. His words (theory) will recast the new in the forms of the old and where he finds discrepancies (differences) he gives his greatest attention. This allows the critic to conclude that cubist painters were doing something to perspective, or that concrete poets were doing something to syntax. Not so.

An examination of cubist painting and concrete poetry in terms of their effect on perspective and syntax is not a study of painting and poetry; rather, it is a study of criticism, of social history and of a language that is not the language of art.

For ______ 15 July, 1991.

(Your words) "What happens to painting, or visual images generally, when they get talked about, that is, when they are made to enter into language..."

(My comment) If you discuss what you see represented in a representational painting, you will formulate a theory about the thing represented. If you discuss whatever you think is *implied* by the visual, you will be *inventing* a narrative. A painting, it is said, can be understood on many levels. These levels are invented by the viewer, not by the painter, nor are they directly relevant to the painting being viewed.

(Your words) "... language has the power to *appropriate* the visual... criticism *narrativizes* painting."

(My comment) Not so. Talk is talk; these ideas will make your work, not a study of painting, but a study of talk. Painting does not enter language when it is talked about. The painting remains, endures, while talk goes on around it and when all of the talk is done, still there is the painting.

I still believe that we are less in agreement than you think we are. Our arguments stem from a fundamental difference in our thinking. I do not accept "language" as a name for the visual phenomenon of painting.

I believe that painting *communicates.* When Kahnweiler wrote that painting is writing (or, *a kind of* writing) he was using metaphor. The metaphor makes one point: *painting is a kind of writing because, like writing, it communicates.* Beyond this the metaphor does not hold up; it was not an analogy. If, with your view of language and writing, you are going to insist that painting *is* writing, there will be great arguments ahead.

Barbara

9 September, 1991.

Dear ______

Your letter helps me see where our agreement and disagreement lie. It is in the *difference* between painting and writing. Paintings are visual; they report *to* the viewer's eye and mind. Writing elicits a report *from* the reader's mind. That difference begins to close with poetry, in particular with visual and concrete poetry. The see/know that I have tried to emphasize in my writing to you can also be written— bp did it in *Continental Trance.*

(Your words) "What painting brings to language is... a silence... within the realm of the sign (that *is* an apple, that *is* Mont Ste. Victoire)..."

(My comment) I have to challenge what you've put in brackets. No, that is not an apple, it's paint, it's colour, a configuration of coloured marks that *remind you of* that thing that you have seen before, called "apple."

I will try to explain my resistance to your idea. I think that Cézanne would want you to be reminded of an apple when you looked at his painting. He would want you to see *all that he had made*. I suspect that he would use the word "apple" himself, but that fact does not enforce a "linguistic imperialism" over painting. Cézanne would want you to *notice*, consciously, that his strokes of colour were *not* an apple as you had ever previously seen it, and *not* an apple as you had ever previously seen one painted. He would be disappointed if you were not conscious of that, were not *arrested* by it, *astounded* by it. What he might think he had done for you (the viewer) is given you a new experience of colour and light. He might think that you, after seeing his painting, will never see an apple in nature again as you saw it before you saw his painting— he has given you his vision, a new seeing. (I don't believe that a viewer completes a painting; rather, it is more accurate to say that the painting completes the viewer by adding to his vision, his visual experience.)

Cézanne was not accepted by the Academy. It was because he did not make "apples" that *looked like* all the other "apples" that had been painted before. His paintings were rejected because they didn't follow the established *code*, because he did not render *signs* in the conventional manner. Cézanne exploded vision and consciousness, and it made *painting* of painting. Cézanne saw all painting as *painting*— that's why he wanted to redo (as painting) all of the paintings in the museums. After Cézanne, all of the paintings in the museums were seen anew. Cézanne did it.

So why are you still talking about "apples"?

When you say that "painting enters language," it reminds me of that Academy that rejected Cézanne. It classifies painting as writing, as code, as sign. Some paintings are made to incite, sometimes confound, the mind of the viewer. Similarities to familiar objects allude to the viewer's memory setting him on a path of self-absorbed thought. (Surrealists like Dali, Ernst or Magritte do this.) But even these paintings *work* (action); the concrete elements must be right or the painting won't capture (arrest) or evoke a re-action in the viewer. The active elements in painting are *abstract*. They serve what is represented in the painting only when they are present and complete in themselves. With them, the painting is called "good"; without them, it is called "bad." This is true in modernist painting.

Post-modern painting, especially the painting of the 1980s, is figurative (representational). It is classified as "expressionist," "neo-expressionist" and "surrealist"— these old words are applied to this new painting— and those abstract elements which are so hard to describe are considered irrelevant. This has allowed *bad* painting to become "good" painting, and it is the preferred form. Visual consciousness has been set aside. The elements of post-modern painting are metaphors and the painting is "discourse." In it, colour is symbol and image is sign. These paintings are to be viewed as coded messages that are to be de-coded by the viewer. In this way, it can be said that the viewer completes the painting. *Interpretation* (or criticism) has superseded painting— here is your "linguistic imperialism"!

Post-modern painting has to be interpreted and all interpretations are valid. So artists are painting, collaging, drawing stuff and appropriating things for viewers to recognize, name and extrapolate on by interpretation. This is *critical art*. Language plays a dominant role in this art. Philosophical models from Barthes to Derrida have given rise to theories about painting as *language*.

I have been looking at a lot of this art. It was the "trend" of the 1980s and it continues today. I would have no argument with it if painting as *painting* had not been made the first casualty of its language-war. [Abstract or concrete painting is not *coded*, therefore, no one can *de-code* it!] I am interested in the literary models that are being used to interpret painting. They are clever, but they seem limited to examining only one aspect of thought, that aspect that expresses itself in words. This is not because all painter's *word* their paintings, but because all critics *word* their criticism. Linguistic imperialism currently prevails; it is the critic who has the power in what you have said is "the only game in town."

You write that you are unable to believe that anything exists outside language, "... but if it does, I have no way of knowing it, no way of talking about it." I am disturbed to read this. What I have called "see/know" can be talked about. Language may indeed take the bait, but language may also fail— it fails because the *bait* is not language. If the bait *is* language, then language has itself by the tail (and we know just how far it will get *that* way.)

Barbara

24 September, 1991.

Dear ______

I received your letter and your postcard.[1]

I will try to write down my understanding of this passage. I suspect we have different interpretations. To me, these words confirm my side of the debate; you probably sent them to point out that your side (the undeniable "apple") is supported by them.

In the first sentence, Stein classifies the painted image using metaphor and simile ("The apples [metaphor] looked *like* apples..."), then denies that with "it all had nothing to do with anything...") I think Stein is saying: "the [painted] apples looked like apples [the familiar object]... and it [the painting]... had nothing to do with anything [any thing— not apples]."

Then, Stein confirms: "because if they did not look like apples... they were apples..." The metaphor is confirmed, but not the image. Stein has noticed that the painted "apples" do not imitate the object (apple) in appearance. She upholds the metaphor because she is restricted by language.

Stein has said "yes" and "no" to the metaphor, then she says "yes" again: "they were so entirely these things... not an oil painting..." and she denies the painting. Then she confirms it, "and yet... they were an oil painting."

I think Stein's yes/no/yes/no/yes effectively uses language to address what is outside language. It is not equivocation. Stein does not try to conceal; rather, she brings opposing ideas together (ideas rooted in language) to express something that is *outside* of language.

What we call apples, chairs, landscape or people exist outside of language. The things so named, like a painting, are real and concrete. We name them to classify them, to separate them into general categories and agree that certain words have certain meanings. We create a vocabulary in common so we can talk together.

We talk words— a language. We do not talk painting (as we talk/speak French or English). We talk *about* painting (about as if around), but our words cannot make or change a painting— it endures, remains, is not affected by all of the talk that goes on about it or around it.

Words *may* affect those viewers of the painting who are more able to grasp concepts, however general, through language than they can grasp their own perception. For them, the word "apple" has more meaning than does the encounter of the eye with redness, and it will be reassuring for those viewers to name that redness (or yellowness) "apple." But the redness does not change. When the redness is perceived to be "apple," it is made to conform, in the viewer's mind, to aspects of that object that do not, cannot, exist in a painting. What *does* exist in the painting is easily overlooked or ignored because the viewer has been sidetracked by a *word*.

I have no quarrel with Stein saying, "The apples looked like apples..." but I am disappointed when a viewer concludes that the painting has to do with apples, or says "that *is* an apple," instead of "it all had nothing to do with anything," the way Stein did.

Stein describes the paintings as "finished or unfinished." This is of particular interest to me. She may be referring to those areas in Cézanne's paintings where the canvas ground is left exposed and she is calling the painting "unfinished" because of it. Until Cézanne, only a sketch or an unfinished painting showed exposed ground. With Cézanne (and after), a painting that was finished showed exposed ground with purpose and meaning. You will find canvas ground or white ground exposed in paintings from Picasso to David Milne, in paintings by Frank Stella, Kenneth Noland and Morris Louis— even Josef Albers and (humbly) in my work, too. The exposed ground reveals and confirms the two-dimensional plane as surface. That visible plane (canvas or white ground) is an active part of the completed work. It attests to the material and meaning of the painting, which is "... essentially, a flat plane on which colours have been arranged in a particular order."

Stein is emphatic: "Finished or unfinished it *always* was what it looked like [that is] the very essence of an oil painting because everything was *always* there, *really* there…" I emphasize "always" (enduring, time) and "really" (the stuff of paint).

The last line says that with this experience and understanding of Cézanne's painting as *painting* (outside language), Stein is made confident to begin her writing. Stein's writing (inside language) is a writing that addresses and acknowledges what is outside language.

I love the poets.

I look forward to reading your drafts for the first chapters of your book.

Barbara

Notes:

1. The postcard showed a reproduction of Cézanne's *Still Life with Apples and Cake* and on the message side, ______ had written this passage by Gertrude Stein:

> The apples looked like apples the chairs looked like chairs and it all had nothing to do with anything because if they did not look like apples or chairs or landscape or people they were apples and chairs and landscape and people. They were so entirely these things that they were not an oil painting and yet that is just what the Cézannes were they were an oil painting. They were so entirely an oil painting that it was all there whether they were finished, the paintings, or whether they were not finished. Finished or unfinished it always was what it looked like the very essence of an oil painting because everything was always there, really there… This then was a great relief to me and I began my writing.

Letter to an Art Critic.

(Excerpt.)

7 December, 1991.

Dear ______ ______

I have read the pages in Fernande Saint-Martin's *Semiotics of Visual Language* that deal with Musatti, and with Kanizsa and the "Musatti effect." You will remember that this "effect" was the only aspect of your essay on my paintings that I questioned when we spoke on the phone.

I'm still of the opinion that the "Musatti effect" is not relevant to my work. In your essay, you have said that the loose-edged shapes and the fine line of bled colour at the boundary of each shape create a "boundary variable" where it meets the canvas ground. You classify the boundaries (of the colour-shapes and of the exposed canvas ground) as diffuse, rather than distinct; this is to my mind an error. To interpret this as a condition of the Musatti effect is to misconstrue what is actually at work in the painting. Your comment on the extreme subtlety of the effect would indicate that the optical experience is not immediate, in fact, that it is slight, but it may occur if a viewer is seeking it.

When I read this part of the essay, I believed that you wanted to account for the exposure of the canvas. In the painting, the canvas ground is coloured; the paint has been applied thinly so the weave and texture of the canvas is clearly visible. The materiality of the work, its coloured canvas ground and the skin of dense opaque paint applied to it to form each colour-shape, is clearly visible. *Materiality* is a self-evident fact of the work. The colour-shapes are distinct and show a clear boundary. The shapes do not abut, but give evidence of their material by the bled edges which grip the material of the canvas whether it is coloured (as in this painting) or in its natural state. The *material presence* of the work is understood by these visible events.

It is difficult to argue this question with you because we are talking about an *optical* effect— I can't deny that you experienced it. Optical effects occur in the eye and mind of the viewer and they are usually the consequence of certain conditions established in the work by the artist. Throughout all of the Colour Lock paintings, I did not want to create conditions that would invite illusory responses. On the contrary, I made works that do not conceal any aspect of their behaviour; they are paint and canvas— real, concrete and visible.

I do not want to challenge your experience of the painting, but I am concerned that you have misrepresented my work in your essay. The passage about the Musatti effect is misleading. It may encourage viewers hereafter to overlook the real material aspects of my paintings (these, too, are phenomenal) and instead, to suspend reality in search of this optical effect.

Barbara Caruso

Acknowledgements

"The Toronto Art Scene" appeared as "A Letter from Paris" in *Work Seen* Vol. 1, No. 1. Summer 1989.

"Artists' Writing and Critics' Writing" appeared as "A Letter from Paris" in *Work Seen* Vol. 1, No. 2. September-October 1989.

"The Costakis Collection" appeared as "A Letter from Paris" in *Work Seen* Vol. 1, No. 3. November- December 1989.

"*Abstraction-Geometry-Painting*. The exhibition" appeared as "A Letter from Paris" in *Work Seen* Vol. 1, No. 4. March 1990.

"*Abstraction-Geometry-Painting*. The catalogue" appeared as "A Letter from Paris" in *Work Seen* No. 5. Spring-Summer 1990.

"*Voice of Fire*. The controversy" appeared as "A Letter from Paris" in *Work Seen* No. 6. September 1990.

"*Voice of Fire*. The painting" appeared as "A Letter from Paris" in *Work Seen* No. 7. December 1990-January 1991.

"The Myth of the Artist's Five-Year Career" appeared as "A Letter from Paris" in *Work Seen* No. 8. Spring 1991.

"Nancy Davidson's *Untitled: For Margaret Mead*" appeared in *Artists Review* 2/9 1979.

"The Canada Council Art Bank Exhibition at I.G.A. Gallery" appeared in *Artmagazine* 58/59. May/June/July 1982.

"Vera Frenkel's *In Search Of The True Blue Romance*" appeared in *Artmagazine* 60. September/October 1982.

"8 ARTPARK Projects" appeared in *C magazine* No. 2. Summer 1984.

"Who Are You, Greg Curnoe?" appeared in *Work Seen* Vol.1, No. 4. March 1990.

"Guido Molinari: The Formative Years" appeared in *Work Seen* No. 6. September 1990.

"The Robert Downing Archive" appeared in *Work Seen* No. 12. Spring 1992.

What Colour Are The Gallery Walls? was privately printed and circulated by the author to 130 individuals from November 1996 to Summer 1998.

"Telling About Line Telling" appeared in *Open Letter* Second Series, No. 5. Summer 1973. Issue on Narrative. [TRG report 2]

"Paintings 1969-1977" appeared in the catalogue for the exhibition at the Gallery/Stratford, Ontario, in May 1977.

"The Colour Lock Paintings 1969-1983" appeared in *Open Letter* Sixth Series, No. 4: Spring 1986. Issue on Barbara Caruso.

"Small Paintings" accompanied the exhibition at The Manning Gallery, Toronto, in November 1986.

"Point to Line to Plane: Drawings 1973-1985" appeared on the announcement for the exhibition at the Kitchener-Waterloo Art Gallery in June-July 1988.

"Working Notes and Drawings" appeared in the group exhibition, *Working Notes and Drawings*, curated by Catherine Carmichael, at Extension Gallery, Toronto, in February 1991. My contribution was a photocopy of my hand-written journal entries and the sketches and trial drawings for *Plane Shapes: Bound and Unbound #1-6*.

"Primal Colour Paintings" appeared in the catalogue for the exhibition at Workscene Gallery, Toronto, in November 1991.

"Colour/Shape/Surface: small paintings and drawings 1987-88" appeared in the catalogue for the exhibition at Blackwood Gallery, Erindale College, Mississauga, in February 1994.

"Paintings 1990-91 and Drawings 1984 & 1990" appeared in the catalogue for the exhibition at The Library & Gallery, Cambridge, Ontario, in June-July 1996.

"Serial Works: paintings and drawings" appeared in the catalogue for the exhibition at Artword Gallery, Toronto, in October-November 1999.

"Reds, Yellows, Blues, Blacks and Whites" appeared in the catalogue for the exhibition at Artword Gallery, Toronto, in October-November 2000.

Index of Persons